The Value of Life

AN ECONOMIC ANALYSIS

The Value of Life.

AN ECONOMIC ANALYSIS

M. W. Jones-Lee

The University of Chicago Press
Chicago

The University of Chicago Press, Chicago 60637
Martin Robertson & Co., London N1 8HL

Published 1976

Printed in Great Britain

Library of Congress Cataloging in Publication Data
Jones-Lee, M W
    The value of life.

    1. Life expectancy — Cost effectiveness. 2. Safety
regulations — Cost effectiveness. 3. Insurance, Life —
Cost effectiveness. 4. Uncertainty. I. Title.
HB199.J64 1976   301.32'2   76-7395
ISBN 0-226-40794-2

Contents

v

Preface

Allocative decision-making in the public sector, if it is to be anything other than purely haphazard, requires consistent and clearly specified procedures for placing values upon the various desirable and undesirable effects of an adjustment in the way scarce resources are utilised. By and large the general principles for deriving such values are well established. However, there remain certain notable problems that are, as yet, essentially unresolved. Prominent among these is the question of the appropriate procedure for placing a value on an anticipated reduction in the mortality (or non-fatal accident) rate owing to public expenditure designed to increase safety or longevity. The problem has typically been posed as that of discovering the 'value of human life (and limb)', the philosophical ferocity of this question making it abundantly clear why no consensus has emerged concerning an answer.

This book has two primary objectives. The first is to pose the question of the value of life and safety improvement (or reduction) in a form that makes it amenable to analysis using the conceptual apparatus of economic theory (especially that provided by the theory of choice under uncertainty). The second major objective is to develop an analytical framework within which the question, having been appropriately formulated, can then be answered, first at a qualitative and then at a quantitative level.

The book contains seven chapters. Chapter 1 presents a brief outline of the conventional procedures of public sector allocative decision-making, special consideration being given to the fundamental rationale for cost—benefit analysis. Chapter 2 surveys the existing literature in the 'value of life' and 'safety improvement' field and evaluates each contribution with particular reference to its relevance for cost—benefit analysis. Chapter 3 contains a brief exposition of those aspects of the theory of choice under uncertainty that are particularly important for later chapters. Chapter 4 examines the individual's decision concerning expenditure on life insurance, emphasis being placed upon the necessary and sufficient conditions for the purchase of such insurance to be desirable from the individual's point of view. These conditions then play an important part in the development, in chapter 5, of a number of qualitative results concerning the value of changes in safety and longevity.

Chapter 6 outlines an experimental procedure for obtaining quantitative estimates of the value of changes in safety and reports the results of a limited number of such experiments. Finally, chapter 7 surveys the arguments of the preceding chapters, explores strengths and weaknesses and offers suggestions for future research.

An attempt has been made to build up the technical (and particularly the mathematical) complexity of the argument in a gradual manner. Thus while chapters 1 and 2 are practically devoid of mathematical content, chapters 3, 4 and 5 do make fairly extensive use of more formal analytical techniques. It should be stressed, however, that while some of the mathematical expressions in chapters 3, 4 and 5 look a little forbidding, the essential ideas underlying these expressions should be accessible (and, indeed, familiar) to the majority of well trained undergraduates.

My interest in the 'value of life' and the 'value of safety' was originally generated by a paper on cost—benefit analysis read to the York graduate economic theory seminar by Alan Williams some time during 1968. I am particularly grateful for this initial stimulus and for subsequent discussion, encouragement and criticism.

A slightly later (but no less valuable) commentary on my ideas came from Alan Peacock, whose suggestions have led to a number of insights.

Jack Wiseman and Ron Cooper supervised the preparation of my doctoral thesis at York. Since part of this thesis was concerned with the 'value of safety' problem, many of the ideas that appear in this book were tempered between the poles of Jack Wiseman's well-known involvement in the *subjective* view of costs and Ron Cooper's equally strong attachment to the *objective* view of probability. Ribaldry apart, both have been immensely helpful and encouraging over the years.

Jacques Drèze and Jim Mirrlees, together with the other organisers and participants at the 1971 International Economics Association Theory Workshop held in Bergen, gave extremely valuable commentary and constructive criticism of an early draft of my *JPE* paper upon which chapter 5 is based.

Tony Culyer, David Gowland and Jim Malcomson have made many valuable comments and suggestions.

Gavin Mooney, John Lawson and David Benson have each been involved in various ways with empirical aspects of the 'value of safety' problem and have therefore had a substantial influence upon the formation of my ideas.

Finally, a large number of people (whose names I simply cannot remember) have made fruitful criticisms and suggestions during seminars and discussions involving aspects of the material presented in this book. I am most grateful to all of these people.

1. Allocative Decision-Making in the Public Sector

The purpose of this book is to consider the closely related questions of the value of life and the value of safety. Quite apart from their intrinsic interest and novelty, these questions are clearly of fundamental importance for most public investment decisions in the health and transport fields and also have substantial (if less direct) relevance for a wide variety of other allocative decisions in the public sector.

In considering the typical health or transport investment programme the public decision-making body must somehow weigh and evaluate the variety of desirable and undesirable effects that the programme can be expected to generate. How are changes in mortality rates and in safety to be handled in this process? Are such effects by their very nature incapable of being evaluated within the same decision-making calculus as, say, savings in time or changes in the availability of raw materials? The purpose of this book is to consider such questions and to develop an analytical framework within which one may discuss the value of changes in safety in a manner consistent with established procedures commonly adopted in allocative and investment decision-making in the public sector. Given this objective, it is obviously desirable to begin our discussion by outlining the underlying principles of those public sector allocative decision-making procedures that are commonly adopted.

Without doubt the most important and most commonly employed procedure of allocative decision-making in the public sector is *cost—benefit analysis*. Superficially this analytical device closely resembles the well established 'project selection' techniques employed by firms pursuing some version of the 'shareholder wealth maximisation' goal; that is, a time-stream of net benefits — typically expressed as money values — is discounted for futurity and compared with a capital outlay. If the discounted net benefit stands in some prespecified relation to capital outlay (e.g. exceeds capital outlay) then the project is recommended: otherwise it is rejected. The more sophisticated versions of this procedure give explicit recognition to the fact that future time-streams of benefits are necessarily subject to uncertainty, and a variety of devices has been adopted to allow the nature and degree of uncertainty to be explicitly reflected in the final decision.

The resemblance between cost—benefit analysis and 'commercial' project appraisal is, however, more apparent than real. This is hardly surprising since the ultimate objectives of public-sector decision-makers are unlikely to bear much resemblance to the objectives of decision-makers in the private sector. The essential difference is that the managers of a firm will probably be largely concerned with their own and their shareholders' interests (both sets of interests typically being intimately dependent upon the aggregate value of the firm's equity shares[1]) while the public-sector decision-maker normally will be concerned with a more nebulous index of the welfare of society 'as a whole' (including himself). As a consequence 'net benefits' are usually synonymous with 'net profit' in commercial project appraisal, whereas the constitutents and character of net benefits in cost—benefit analysis are altogether more problematic and controversial.

A similar divergence of conceptual difficulty is associated with discounting procedures in the two types of project appraisal. It is fairly clear that a firm attempting to maximise the market value of its equity shares need discover only the manner in which the capital market implicitly discounts the future flow of net revenues of the firm and then employ similar discounting procedures in evaluating new capital investment. The public decision-maker, on the other hand, has no such straightforward prescription. Variation in the timing of net benefits affects different generations. How are the interests of each generation to be weighed and compared? If resources are diverted from the private to the public sector then some private-sector investment will typically be forgone. Should the public-sector discounting procedure somehow reflect the rate of return on this forgone private-sector investment? Should the public decision-maker simply 'take a view' on the optimal time path of consumption and let the discounting procedure reflect this view or should he, in contrast, take current individual preferences over consumption through time as the primary determinant of the public sector discount rate by basing the latter on market rates of interest in the private sector? These questions and many besides have troubled those concerned with the problem of discounting in cost—benefit analysis. Many of the issues are still unresolved and almost certainly by their nature irresolvable.[2]

I COST—BENEFIT ANALYSIS, CITIZENS' SOVEREIGNTY AND THE 'POTENTIAL PARETO IMPROVEMENT' CRITERION

Clearly, the key to the central conceptual problems of cost—benefit analysis is the nature of the ultimate objectives of the public-sector decision-maker.[3] A clear and precise statement of these objectives would undoubtedly go a long way to resolve the problems outlined above. Unfortunately, however, it would be naive in the extreme to suppose that decision-makers in the public sector regularly and consistently behave in a manner capable of being described as the pursuit of a single or even a limited set of clearly defined goals. This reservation notwithstanding, unless the decision-maker is taken to display *some* regularity and consistency of choice, then there will be practically nothing of a general nature to be said about cost—benefit analysis. It is therefore normally assumed that in that limited aspect of his role involving decisions concerning the allocation of scarce resources, the public decision-maker at least behaves in a manner that is consistent with the following precept:

If no individual's welfare is lower under allocation X than under allocation Y and some individuals' welfare is higher under X than under Y, then allocation X is better than allocation Y. (In all but exceptional circumstances,[4] the necessary and sufficient condition for an *individual's* welfare to be greater under allocation X than under allocation Y is that the individual *himself* should prefer X to Y.)

This precept or ethical prescription is generally known as the condition of 'citizens' sovereignty', or alternatively as the 'Paretian value judgement' after its original proponent Vilfredo Pareto.[5]

Now even supposing that for all allocative decisions it is possible to predict each individual's judgement concerning effects upon his own welfare, it is clear that the Paretian value judgement merely permits an ordering *within subsets* of allocations, each subset being such that for any two allocations Z and W in the subset, if anyone's welfare is greater (lower) in Z than in W then no one's welfare is lower (greater) in Z than in W. Since the majority of decisions will involve comparison of allocations from *different* subsets — and the Paretian value judgement implies nothing whatsoever about orderings over such allocations — any worthwhile public allocative decision-making procedures must obviously be based upon ethical judgements *over and above* the condition of citizens' sovereignty. Furthermore, these ethical judgements must, by definition, be such as to allow comparison of allocative changes that improve some people's welfare and detract from others'. That is, the additional value judgements must be essentially *distributional* in character. A set of value judgements sufficiently robust to give an ordering over *all* alternative allocations would therefore be extremely strong and would be hardly likely to have very wide appeal, given the diversity of human preferences and ideologies. As a corollary it seems unlikely that any such set of value judgements could be taken to characterise the allocative decisions of a wide variety of public decision-makers. It is almost certainly for this reason that most proponents of cost—benefit analysis recognise that the desirability of an allocative change will probably ultimately be judged by a number of different criteria, the results of a cost—benefit analysis being only *one* relevant criterion. To put the matter in a slightly different way, cost—benefit analysis has come to be regarded by many of its advocates *not* as a device by which decision-makers may, as it were, derive a *final* ordering over alternative allocations, but rather as a means of ordering allocations in terms of *one* of the many characteristics relevant to a final ordering.[6]

For advocates of this approach (which we shall call the 'restricted' view) the particular characteristic with which cost—benefit analysis is taken to be concerned in considering any allocative adjustment is the extent to which the allocative change can be said to represent a 'potential Pareto improvement'. A change from allocation X to allocation Y generates a potential Pareto improvement if those whose welfare is increased by the change from X to Y gain by a sufficient amount to be able to compensate fully those whose welfare is reduced and still remain better off. Let us call the set of people who either gain or do not lose by the change from X to Y group G and the set of people who lose by the move group L. According to the restricted view, cost—benefit analysis is then effectively concerned with the question of whether there exists any redistribution of wealth from G to L that, following a change from allocation X to allocation Y, would yield a final situation preferable to X *on the basis of the citizens' sovereignty precept*. It must be stressed that the answer to this question is *not* taken to be the sole criterion by which the move from X to Y is to be judged, but is merely held by those who subscribe to this view of cost—benefit analysis to be 'relevant information' for any public decision-maker whose list of ethical judgements includes, among others, the citizens' sovereignty precept. Furthermore it should be emphasised that the potential Pareto improvement criterion involves *no* implicit recommendation about whether or not group G should *actually* compensate group L: on the restricted view this is held to be a matter quite outside the scope of cost—benefit analysis.

Quite apart from its failure to give any indication of the desirability of *actual* compensation, the potential Pareto improvement criterion has a further serious shortcoming that should be noted at this stage. Under certain circumstances it is possible for a change from allocation X to allocation Y to represent a potential Pareto improvement *and* for the change *back* from allocation Y to allocation X also to represent a potential Pareto improvement.[7] In formal terms the relation of 'being potentially Pareto-preferred' is *non-symmetric* rather than *asymmetric* and cannot therefore form the basis for a strong (or 'strict') ordering.[8] This is undoubtedly a distinct disadvantage, but provided that the cost—benefit analyst is aware of the problem and is also careful to point out any instance of its occurrence, then it would not seem to detract *too* severely from the value of the potential Pareto improvement criterion as a decision-making tool.

The first question that arises in applying the potential Pareto improvement criterion concerns the means by which one is to decide whether or not the group that gains by a change from allocation X to allocation Y could or could not compensate the group that loses by the move. In a market economy the procedure is relatively straightforward. One need merely discover the largest amount of generalised purchasing power (i.e. money income) that could be taken from the gainers after the change from X to Y without making them feel that their welfare had been reduced below its original level under allocation X. Suppose that this amount of money income *exceeds* the minimum amount of money income that the losers would require to be given in conjunction with the change from X to Y so as to make them feel that their welfare had not been reduced below its original level under allocation X. Then clearly the type of compensation specified in the potential Pareto improvement criterion *could* be effected. The maximum amount gainers would forfeit and the minimum sum losers would require in compensation have come to be known[9] as 'compensating variations' in income (or wealth) so that the condition[10] for a potential Pareto improvement may be stated as the existence of a positive *aggregate*[11] compensating variation in income (a gainer's hypothetical forfeit being treated as a *positive* compensating variation and a loser's hypothetical compensation being treated as a *negative* compensating variation).[12] Alternatively, if we call the maximum sum gainers would forfeit the 'benefits' generated by the allocative change and the minimum sum losers would require in compensation the 'costs' owing to the allocative change *then the condition for a potential Pareto improvement may be stated as an excess of benefits over costs.* (This affords a natural and intuitively appealing definition for the concepts of 'benefit' and 'cost' in the context of cost—benefit analysis.) *Notice that there is nothing special about using money income in this exercise.* Suppose that, instead, one wished to conduct the analysis using, say, apples as the standard of comparison. If the ith gainer is prepared to forfeit an amount m_i of money income to effect the change from X to Y then, by definition, he would instead be prepared to forfeit m_i *times* his marginal rate of substitution of apples for income in order to effect the change.[13] Similarly if the jth loser requires an amount m_j in compensation for the change then he would instead accept m_j *times* his marginal rate of substitution of apples for income. However, in a market economy, with all individuals employing chosen expenditure patterns, each individual's marginal rate of substitution of apples for income will equal the inverse of the price of apples.[14] Thus

$$\sum_i m_i > \sum_j m_j$$

is the *necessary and sufficient* condition for the amount of apples gainers would forfeit to *exceed* the amount of apples losers would require in compensation.

Finally, it is worth noting that any allocative adjustment that is an *actual* Pareto improvement (i.e. is recommended by the citizen's sovereignty precept) also necessarily passes the potential Pareto improvement test.

II   ESTIMATION OF COMPENSATING VARIATIONS IN INCOME

Having established the general principle by which a particular allocative adjustment might be judged to represent a potential Pareto improvement, it is then necessary to specify the procedure by which one might discover the magnitude of compensating variations in income for those who gain and lose by the allocative adjustment. The ease with which the compensating variations may be discovered depends, not surprisingly, upon the nature of the allocative change involved. We can fruitfully distinguish four cases of varying complexity:

(a) variation in the output of a commodity for which there exists a market: no externalities[15] in consumption or production; no consequent variation in the price of other commodities or factors;[16]

(b) variation in the output of a marketed commodity: no externalities in consumption or production; *consequent variation in the prices of other commodities or factors*;

(c) variation in the output of a marketed commodity: *externalities in consumption or production*; no consequent variations in prices of other commodities or factors;

(d) *variation in the output of a commodity for which no market exists:* no consequent variations in prices of other commodities or factors.

Consider the first alternative. Suppose that the market demand curve for the commodity is as depicted by the curve *DD* in figure 1.1. Before the allocative change output q_x is sold at price p_x while after the change output q_y is sold at price p_y.

To each point on *DD* there corresponds what is known as an 'income-compensated' (or more briefly, a 'compensated') demand curve showing the aggregate amount that would be demanded at each price if all consumers' incomes were varied *in conjunction with price changes* so as to leave every consumer indifferent between his positions before and after the price change. On the assumption that the commodity in question is not an 'inferior'[17] good, the income-compensated demand curve corresponding to the point (q_x, p_x) on *DD* will be as depicted by the chain-dotted curve $D_x D_x$.[18] It is a well established result[19] that (provided all other prices are constant) consumers' aggregate compensating variation for a reduction in price from p_x to p_y is given by the area bounded by the price axis, the ordinates p_x and p_y and the income-compensated demand curve $D_x D_x$ (i.e. by the shaded area in figure 1.1). Since there are by

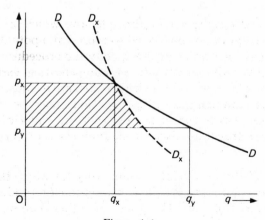

Figure 1.1.

assumption no externalities and no other price changes, the only other relevant compensating variations are those of producers of the commodity and suppliers of factors of production used in producing the commodity. That is, we must also consider variations in producers' and factor suppliers' rents. By assumption, no other factor or product prices vary so that there will be no variation in rents of *factor* suppliers. However, *producers* of the commodity whose output changes will in general experience some variation in rent (i.e. a change in supernormal profit) as a result of the variation in output and this must be added to (or subtracted from) the aggregate compensating variation of consumers in order to decide whether or not the allocative change implies a potential Pareto improvement.

Let us now consider the situation in which there is some variation in the prices of other commodities or factors as a consequence of variation in the output of the commodity under consideration (which will be referred to in what follows as commodity 1). Consider first the case in which the price of only *one* other commodity (say commodity 2) changes, and suppose for the sake of argument that this commodity is a gross substitute[20] for commodity 1. We shall illustrate the procedure for establishing consumers' aggregate compensating variation by considering a change from allocation X to allocation Y involving a simultaneous *reduction* in the prices of both commodities from p_{1x} and p_{2x} to p_{1y} and p_{2y}. The initial position of the demand curves for the two commodities and initial prices and quantities demanded are shown in figure 1.2.

Consider the following sequence of *hypothetical* changes. First suppose that the price of commodity 1 is reduced from p_{1x} to p_{1y} *with the price of commodity 2 held constant at p_{2x}*. This change will leave the position of $D_1 D_1$ unaltered but will shift $D_2 D_2$ to a new

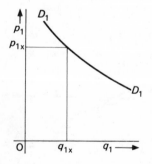
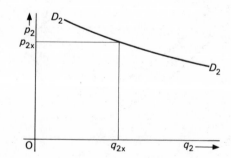

Figure 1.2.

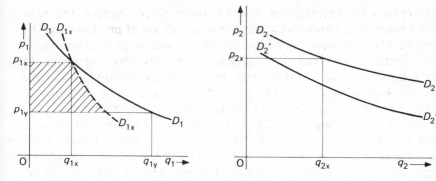

Figure 1.3.

position $D_2'D_2'$ as depicted in figure 1.3. Consumers' aggregate compensating variation for this isolated price change will, of course, be given by the shaded area in figure 1.3 bounded by the relevant income-compensated demand curve for commodity 1. This aggregate compensating variation will be denoted by V_1.

Now let each consumer's income be reduced by the appropriate compensating variation for the isolated price change from p_{1x} to p_{1y} (The sum of these *individual* compensating variations will, by definition, be V_1.) As each individual's income is reduced by the appropriate compensating variation, so the demand curves for both commodities will shift inward[21] to positions $D_1'D_1'$ and $D_2''D_2''$ as depicted in figure 1.4.

Finally, starting from the situation depicted in figure 1.4, let the price of commodity 2 be reduced from p_{2x} to p_{2y} *with the price of commodity 1 held constant at* p_{1y}. This change will leave the position of $D_2''D_2''$ unaltered but will shift $D_1'D_1'$ inward to $D_1''D_1''$ as depicted in figure 1.5.

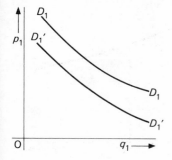
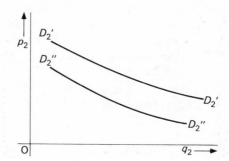

Figure 1.4.

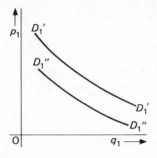 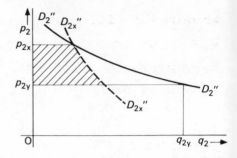

Figure 1.5.

With aggregate income already reduced by V_1 following the first price change, the aggregate compensating variation for the second price change — which will be denoted V_2 — is (by the now familiar argument) given by the shaded area in figure 1.5 bounded by the relevant income-compensated demand curve for commodity 2.

Let us denote consumers' initial aggregate income by I. By the definition[22] of V_1 it then follows that consumers are *indifferent* between, on the one hand, allocation X (their initial position characterised by prices p_{1x} and p_{2x} and aggregate income I) and, on the other hand, allocation Z (the situation in which prices are p_{1y} and p_{2x} and aggregate income has been reduced to $I - V_1$). Similarly, by the definition of V_2 it follows that consumers are indifferent between, on the one hand, allocation Z and, on the other hand, allocation W[23] (the situation in which prices are p_{1y} and p_{2y} and aggregate income has been further reduced to $I - V_1 - V_2$). However, if consumers are indifferent between allocations X and Z and are also indifferent between allocations Z and W, then it follows from transitivity of the indifference relation that they are also indifferent between allocations X and W. Consumers' aggregate compensating variation for the combined price change from p_{1x} and p_{2x} to p_{1y} and p_{2y} is therefore given by $V_1 + V_2$.

The result for the general case involving variation in the prices of many commodities follows by a similar argument and can most easily be stated by denoting consumers' aggregate compensating variation for a change in an n-dimensional price vector from p_x to p_y with initial aggregate income I[24] as $V(I, p_x \to p_y)$. Then in general,

$$V(I, p_x \to p_y) = \sum_{i=1}^{n} V_i \qquad (1.1)$$

where the V_i ($i = 1 \ldots n$) are defined as follows:

$$V_1 = V[I, (p_{1x}, p_{2x}, \ldots p_{nx}) \rightarrow (p_{1y}, p_{2x}, \ldots p_{nx})] \tag{1.2}$$

$$V_2 = V[I - V_1, (p_{1y}, p_{2x}, \ldots p_{nx}) \rightarrow (p_{1y}, p_{2y}, \ldots p_{nx})] \tag{1.3}$$

$$V_3 = V[I - V_1 - V_2, (p_{1y}, p_{2y}, p_{3x}, \ldots p_{nx}) \rightarrow$$
$$(p_{1y}, p_{2y}, p_{3y}, p_{4x}, \ldots p_{nx})] \tag{1.4}$$

etc.

As in the earlier case, in which only one commodity price changed as a result of the allocative adjustment, it is necessary to add changes in producer rent (i.e. changes in supernormal profit) to the aggregate consumers' compensating variation. However we must now *also* consider the possibility of variation in the prices of factors of production. If the factors concerned are *produced* then again one need merely *add* the further change in factor producers' rents to aggregate consumers' compensating variation *plus* any changes in commodity producers' rents. On the other hand, if the relevant factors are primary and supplied by factor owners who have initial 'endowments' of these factors, then the situation is somewhat more complex. Basically the source of the difficulty is that in such cases there will typically exist a 'reservation' demand for the factor in question — that is, factor owners will (*ceteris paribus*) prefer to give up less rather than more of the factor concerned (e.g. consider the work—leisure choice). Suppose that the aggregate supply curve for some primary factor (e.g. labour) is as shown in figure 1.6 and let the initial price of the factor be W_x.

In general, to each point on SS there will correspond an 'income-compensated' (or 'compensated') supply curve showing the aggregate amount that factor owners would wish to supply at each price if all suppliers' incomes were varied in conjunction with price changes so as to leave every supplier indifferent between his positions before and after the price change. If the factor concerned is not an inferior good then the income-compensated supply curve corresponding to the point (q_x, w_x) on SS will be as depicted by the chain-dotted curve $S_x S_x$.[25] In the case of, for example, a rise in the factor price from w_x to w_y it can be shown that the aggregate compensating variation for factor suppliers — i.e. the aggregate rise in rent — is given by the shaded area in figure 1.6 bounded by the price axis, the ordinates w_x and w_y and the income-compensated supply curve $S_x S_x$. Any such change in rent for suppliers of primary factors should of course, be added to the sum of consumers' aggregate compensating variations and changes in producer rents.

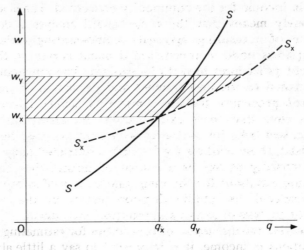

Figure 1.6.

So far nothing has been said about shifts in (produced or primary) factor supply curves caused by commodity price changes or, for that matter, shifts in commodity demand curves caused by (produced or primary) factor price changes. If any such shifts do occur then it is necessary in principle to consider the impact of simultaneous changes in commodity and factor prices in the sequential manner outlined above and formalised in equations (1.1) to (1.4).

Next consider the case in which there are consumption or production externalities associated with variation in the output of the commodity concerned. Very little of a general nature can be said about such effects except that it is necessary, in principle, to include compensating variations for all external benefits and costs that occur. The effectiveness of procedures for obtaining estimates of these compensating variations is largely dependent upon the ingenuity of the cost—benefit analyst, and suffice it to say that the mere identification of externalities associated with any allocative adjustment is often in itself a difficult task.

Finally we turn to the type of allocative adjustment with which this book is primarily concerned, namely a change in the output of a commodity for which no market exists. As in the case of consumption or production externalities there is little of a general nature to be said about such changes except that if cost—benefit analysis *is* taken to be based upon the potential Pareto improvement criterion then, despite the absence of market-generated data, it is nonetheless essential to discover the magnitude of compensating variations in income for the commodity concerned. The absence of a market merely means that the cost—benefit analyst is denied the convenience of measuring aggregate compensating variations by considering areas under compensated demand curves, so that other measurement procedures have to be evolved. The remainder of this book is devoted to the development and discussion of just such a measurement procedure for the commodity 'safety improvement'. While it is clear that there exist markets for safety-improvement devices (e.g. seat belts for motorcar occupants and crash helmets for motorcyclists), these markets are for such a restricted range of goods as to be virtually useless as a source of information concerning compensating variations for the range and variety of safety improvements considered by public decision-makers in the course of cost—benefit analysis of health and transport investment.

Before leaving the discussion of procedures for estimating compensating variations in income, it is important to say a little about how one might in practice set about measuring the relevant areas under income-compensated demand curves, etc. While there do exist fairly well developed econometric techniques for estimating ordinary (i.e. uncompensated) demand functions, there are obvious reasons why it is *not* possible to estimate *compensated* demand functions of the type described above. In view of this difficulty there are two possible lines of attack. One possibility is to make do with the rough approximation given by the area bounded by the relevant price ordinates and the *ordinary* demand curve (i.e. the increase in the traditional 'consumers' surplus'). The quality of this approximation clearly depends upon the magnitude of income effects since the latter determine the extent to which the ordinary and compensated demand curves diverge. Alternatively, one may attempt to estimate demand functions among whose arguments is an *index of real income*. Since the compensated demand curve and the 'real income-constant' demand curve (each corresponding to a given point on the ordinary demand curve) are closely related,[26] the area bounded by the relevant price ordinates and the 'real income-constant' demand curve will normally provide a far closer approximation to the 'true' compensating variation than the area bounded by the ordinary demand curve.[27]

III   DISCOUNTING PROCEDURES

As was noted above, the selection of an appropriate discounting procedure by which a time-stream of benefits and/or costs may be reduced to a present value is one of the most controversial aspects of cost—benefit analysis. However it would seem that the relatively restricted view of cost—benefit analysis adopted in this book (i.e. as a means of discovering whether or not a particular allocative adjust-ment represents a potential Pareto improvement) implies an unam-biguous and straightforward resolution to the discounting question.

Suppose that the effects of an allocative change will be experi-enced by some individual in two successive time periods, t_1 and t_2, and that the individual's compensating variations in income for the two periods are V_1 and V_2 respectively (i.e. the individual *currently* would be willing to forfeit amounts V_1 in t_1 and V_2 in t_2 in order to effect the allocative change). If the individual's private rate of time-preference between consumption in t_1 and t_2 is ρ, then by definition the individual would be indifferent between, on the one hand, forfeiting V_1 in t_1 and V_2 in t_2 and on the other hand forfeiting a single amount equal to $[V_1 + (V_2/1 + \rho)]$ in t_1.[28] The present value of an individual's time stream of compensating variations is therefore obtained simply by discounting the time stream at the individual's *private* time-preference rate.

Now it is a well established result of capital theory[29] that, given a perfect capital market and abstracting from the problem of uncer-tainty, all individuals will adjust their time-streams of consumption until their private time-preference rates are equal to the market rate of interest. Under such circumstances, then, it would be a straight-forward matter to discount the time-streams of *aggregate* compen-sating variations: one would simply use the *common* private rate of time-preference given by the market rate of interest. However, capital markets are not perfect and the future is uncertain. Under these circumstances it might be argued that individuals will adjust consumption streams until their rates of time-preference between consumption claims of a given degree of risk are equal to market rates of interest on financial instruments of similar risk. If this is so then it would seem that the appropriate discount rate to apply to time-streams of aggregate compensating variations is the market rate of interest on financial instruments of similar risk to the investment project generating the compensating variations.

It must be stressed that this relatively straightforward resolution to the discounting problem holds only if the object of cost—benefit analysis is taken to be the restricted one of discovering whether or not aggregate compensating variations are positive. On the wider interpretation of cost—benefit analysis discussed in the next section, however, it is no longer possible to settle the discounting question in this unequivocal and straightforward manner.

IV   AN ALTERNATIVE VIEW CONCERNING THE FOUNDATIONS OF COST—BENEFIT ANALYSIS

It has been emphasised in preceding sections that, for the purposes of discussion in the remainder of this book, cost—benefit analysis will be treated simply as a device for discovering whether or not a particular allocative adjustment represents a potential Pareto improvement. It must be admitted, however, that this interpretation of the nature and purpose of cost—benefit analysis is not shared by all those who have written on the subject. A grander view of cost—benefit analysis is that it should provide an unambiguous and unequivocal answer to allocative questions.[30]

In this 'olympian' approach to cost—benefit analysis the proposition that the benefits owing to some allocative change outweigh the costs of that change is equivalent to the proposition that the allocative change is, on balance, desirable when judged by *all* the criteria relevant to the social decision-maker concerned. This means of course that, in arriving at aggregate values of benefit and cost, the cost—benefit analyst must judge the allocative change by *all* the relevant criteria. Furthermore he must do so in a manner that permits quantification of benefits and costs in a way that precisely reflects the relative importance placed upon each category of benefit and cost by the social decision-maker. It will, for example, be necessary to resolve the discounting problem mentioned earlier and, in addition, to evolve some procedure for weighting the gains and losses of various groups in society so as to reflect the social decision-maker's views on distributional matters.

It is clear that in this approach both the general character and detailed procedure of the cost—benefit analysis are dependent upon the particular ethical, social and political predispositions of the social decision-maker. It is essentially for this reason that the simpler and more restricted view of cost—benefit analysis has been adopted in this book. The restricted view of cost—benefit analysis advocated here avoids the necessity for the analyst to involve himself intimately in the views and ideology of the social decision-maker and gives the results of the cost—benefit analysis far greater generality than they could possibly possess if the analysis reflected the particular predispositions of some individual or group. A secondary advantage of the restricted view is that, since the procedure of the cost—benefit analysis need not be tailored to the views of any specific social decision-maker, it is more likely that a coherent and consistent body of analytical technique will emerge.

Of course the major *disadvantage* of the restricted view of cost—benefit analysis is that the results of the analysis will normally represent only *part* of the information relevant to any particular allocative decision. Presented with the results of a cost—benefit analysis the social decision-maker will be required to weigh this information in relation to all other factors that he considers relevant to the decision. However, for reasons already indicated, this partial approach seems preferable to the concoction of a piece of analytical *haute-cuisine* whose particular flavour is unlikely to have wide appeal to a diversity of ideological palates.

NOTES

1. It has been argued by Marris (1966) and others that the divorce of ownership and control inherent in the 'joint stock enterprise' form of corporate organisation allows a firm's managers to pursue goals other than pure maximisation of the market value of the firm's equity shares. The extent to which the market value-maximisation objective may be subordinated to other purely self-interested managerial goals depends largely upon the degree of imperfection of the capital market. Nonetheless, even in an imperfect capital market it seems likely that managerial ownership of equity and the threat of takeover will together ensure that managers will at least attempt to maintain the market value of equity at some 'reasonable' level.

2. For a lucid discussion of some of the issues involved in the discounting question see Dasgupta and Pearce (1972), chapter 6.

3. Throughout we shall refer to a *single* public decision-maker. However nothing that is said would be altered if decisions were taken by a group rather than by an individual. This is not to say that group decision-making does not involve problems over and above those encountered in the individual decision-making case: it is simply that we shall not be concerned with these problems in this book.

4. E.g. the case of 'merit wants'. A merit want is, roughly speaking, a good (or dis-good) whose contribution to individual welfare is — in the view of the public decision-maker — misjudged by individuals themselves. For a full discussion of merit wants see Musgrave (1959), p. 13.

5. See Pareto (1897).

6. The most notable advocate of this view is Mishan. See for example Mishan (1971).

7. This possibility was first pointed out by Scitovsky (1941). For a lucid discussion of the problem and the preconditions for its occurrence see Mishan (1960).

8. Every well-behaved preference ordering is a 'strong' ordering (or more accurately a strong 'partial' ordering, if the decision-maker is indifferent between any elements in the choice set). For a discussion of relations and orderings see, for example, Suppes (1957).

9. This terminology seems to be due to Hicks (1944).

10. Strictly speaking, this condition is necessary but *not* sufficient for a potential Pareto improvement. The reason for the lack of sufficiency is that the compensating variation is the amount of income that an individual will forfeit (or require in compensation) *on the assumption that he can then dispose of his remaining income as he chooses.* It is clearly possible (though one suspects typically unlikely) that the aggregate of chosen expenditure patterns may not be compatible with the total quantities of goods, etc., in the new allocation. For a full discussion of this possibility see Boadway (1974).

11. That is, the sum of *positive* compensating variations *less* the sum of *negative* compensating variations.

12. In order to ensure the absence of the paradoxical possibility that allocation Y is potentially Pareto-preferred to allocation X while X is also potentially Pareto-preferred to Y, it is therefore necessary to establish that, if there is a positive aggregate compensating variation associated with the change from X to Y, there is *not* also a positive aggregate compensating variation associated with the change *back* from Y to X. This condition may alternatively be stated in terms of the so-called 'equivalent variation' for the change from X to Y. (An equivalent variation in income is the amount of income that an individual would require in compensation in order to forgo a desirable change or the amount he would forfeit in order to avoid an undesirable change.) Defining the amount that an individual would require in compensation in order to forgo a desirable change as a *positive* equivalent variation, it is clear that an individual's equivalent variation for a change from allocation X to allocation Y is simply equal to *minus* his compensating variation for the change from Y to X. The condition for the absence of a badly-behaved ordering over X and Y may therefore be stated as the requirement that the aggregate compensating and equivalent variations for the change from X to Y should *not* be of opposite signs. In addition, we can say that if the ordering is in fact well-behaved, with, for example, Y potentially Pareto preferred to X but not vice-versa then (ignoring the possibility of *zero*-compensating or equivalent variations) an aggregate equivalent variation test of the relative desirability of two allocations will necessarily give the same result as an aggregate-compensating variation test. It is perhaps worth noting at this stage, however, that if one is concerned to order more than two social states then there are certain advantages associated with the use of the equivalent variation concept. For a detailed development of this argument see Foster and Neuberger (1974).

13. An individual's 'marginal rate of substitution' between a pair of goods is the rate at which one good must be substituted for the other in order that the individual shall remain indifferent. The proposition in the text requires, of course, that all variations are sufficiently small to ensure that the relevant marginal rate of substitution may be treated as being constant.

14. Provided, of course, that all individuals are consumers of apples. This proviso restricts the set of goods that may act as a standard of comparison in such an exercise to those goods that *are* consumed by everyone.

15. Loosely, externalities are gains or losses that occur directly rather than as a consequence of trading through a market mechanism. The classic example is

the external cost imposed upon society by a firm owing to the smoke issuing from its factory chimney. More formally, externalities tend to occur whenever property rights in a good are either non-existent, non-enforceable or non-tradeable so that it is not possible to establish a market in the good.

16. Since a variation in the output of a particular commodity will have no effect upon the prices of other commodities and factors *only* under exceptional circumstances, this particular case can be regarded as other than a curiosum only under the usual conditions held to justify partial equilibrium analysis, namely that other price variations are *negligible*.

17. A good is 'inferior' for some range of income if the quantity of the good demanded *decreases* as income increases (all prices constant) over that range.

18. In the limiting case in which the quantity of the good demanded by each consumer is independent of his income (all 'income effects' are zero), $D_x D_x$ *coincides* with *DD*.

19. See for example Vickrey (1964) p. 72.

20. Commodities i and j are said to be 'gross substitutes' if a *ceteris paribus* rise in the price of i(j) is accompanied by an increase in the quantity of j(i) demanded.

21. Assuming that neither good is inferior. Again in the limiting case in which, for example, all individual income effects for commodity 1 are zero, $D_1{'}D_1{'}$ and $D_1 D_1$ will coincide.

22. Throughout this discussion the term 'consumers are indifferent . . .' is to be interpreted as meaning that 'each individual consumer is indifferent . . .'.

23. This allocation is called W rather than Y because income, as well as prices, has changed.

24. Notice that the distribution of I must also be specified.

25. Once again, in the limiting case in which all individual income effects are zero, $S_x S_x$ and SS will coincide.

26. See for example Friedman (1962) p. 51.

27. The qualification 'normally' is used here because if, for example, all income effects are zero then the ordinary and compensated demand curves will coincide so that *no* approximation will be involved in using the ordinary demand curve.

28. Provided, of course, that V_1 and V_2 are both small in relation to the individual's consumption expenditure in t_1 and t_2.

29. See, for example, Fisher (1954).

30. For a discussion of cost—benefit analysis orientated more closely to the wider rather than the narrower view see for example Williams (1972), Wildavsky (1966) and Weisbrod (1968).

REFERENCES

Boadway, R. W. 'The Welfare Foundations of Cost—Benefit Analysis' *Economic Journal* (December 1974)

Dasgupta, A. K. and Pearce, D. W. *Cost—Benefit Analysis: Theory and Practice* London, Macmillan (1972)

Fisher, I. *The Theory of Interest* New York, Kelley and Millman (1954)

Foster, C. D. and Neuberger, H. L. I. 'The Ambiguity of the Consumer's Surplus Measure of Welfare Change' *Oxford Economic Papers* (March 1974)

Friedman, M. *Price Theory* Chicago, Aldine (1962)

Hicks, J. R. 'The Four Consumers' Surpluses' *Review of Economic Studies* (1943).

Marris, R. *The Economic Theory of 'Managerial Capitalism'* London, Macmillan (1966)

Mishan, E. J. 'A Survey of Welfare Economics 1939—59' *Economic Journal* (June 1960)

Mishan, E. J. *Cost—Benefit Analysis* London, Allen and Unwin (1971)

Musgrave, R. A. *The Theory of Public Finance* New York, McGraw-Hill (1959)

Pareto, V. *Cours d'Economie Politique* Lausanne (1897).

Scitovsky, T. 'A Note on Welfare Propositions in Economics' *Review of Economic Studies* (1941)

Suppes, P. *Introduction to Logic* New York, Van Nostrand Reinhold (1957)

Vickrey, W. *Microstatics* New York, Harcourt Brace and World (1964)

Weisbrod, B. A. 'Income Redistribution Effects and Benefit—Cost Analysis' in S. B. Chase (ed.) *Problems in Public Expenditure Analysis* Washington, Brooking (1968)

Wildavsky, A. 'The Political Economy of Efficiency: Cost—Benefit Analysis, Systems Analysis and Program Budgeting' *Public Administration Review* (December 1966)

Williams, A. 'Cost—Benefit Analysis: Bastard Science and/or Insidious Poison in the Body Politick' *Journal of Public Finance* (August 1972)

2. The Value of Life and Safety Improvement: a Survey

In the first chapter we developed the particular rationale for cost—benefit analysis upon which the discussion in the remainder of this book will be based. The primary purpose of the present chapter is to assess the relevance of existing analyses of the value of life and safety improvement for any cost—benefit analysis consistent with this rationale. Sections I—XII provide brief synopses of some of the more important contributions to the literature in this field; section XIII then develops a critique of these contributions. The reader who is concerned with general issues rather than with detailed analytical points may prefer to proceed directly to section XIII.

I DUBLIN AND LOTKA: *THE MONEY VALUE OF A MAN* (1930)[1]

Dublin and Lotka are primarily concerned to estimate '. . . the value of a man to his dependants, that is to those who have a direct interest in his earnings', this figure being (according to Dublin and Lotka) the amount that the individual ought ideally to aim to cover with life insurance. Despite their preoccupation with optimal insurance expenditures, the authors suggest that their 'value of a man' will also be of use in public investment decision-making, especially in health and hygiene as well as in the determination of court awards for injury and incapacitation.

In seeking the amount that an individual is worth to his dependants, Dublin and Lotka concern themselves only with '. . . practical tangible quantities capable of numerical estimate in dollars and cents', or more specifically with the discounted present value of an individual's *net* future earnings, that is *the difference between the discounted present value of his anticipated future earnings and his anticipated future consumption expenditures.*

However, the authors are careful to point out that, in eschewing the consideration of 'esthetic' and 'sentimental' value, they are nonetheless not

... insensible to the deep significance of valuation, of a kind, given to intangible things. Quite on the contrary, realizing the supreme significance of these intangibles in human affairs, we shall expressly refrain from dealing with such spiritual values by methods wholly unadapted for their measurement.

Using a discount rate of 3½ per cent and taking account of normal age-specific[2] mortality rates, Dublin and Lotka estimate the average[3] discounted present value (at birth) of the net future earnings of an individual whose maximum annual salary is $5000 (earned at about age fifty) to be $9802 (present value of gross earnings, $27,209, *less* present value of consumption, $17,407).

Dublin and Lotka also consider a number of other problems such as the cost of raising children to adolescence, the 'burden of the handicapped and the residual value of impaired lives', 'diseases and the depreciation of the economic value of the individual', and in addition they provide a number of tables and formulae including the present value of net future earnings at various ages for various maximum salaries. However, for present purposes the most interesting aspect of the book, apart from the empirical estimates of the present value of net future earnings, is the chapter surveying contributions to the 'value of life' literature *pre-1930*. Broadly speaking, this literature divides into two groups: that which contains the direct antecedents of Dublin and Lotka's empirical analysis, including the work of Petty,[4] Farr[5] and Lüdtke,[6] the other group comprising more general discussions of the value of a man in the context of the concept of 'human capital', including the work of Smith,[7] Engel,[8] Nicholson,[9] and Marshall.[10]

II REYNOLDS: 'THE COST OF ROAD ACCIDENTS' (1956)[11]

Reynolds argues that there are two distinct categories of cost imposed on the community by road accidents:

1. The pain, fear and suffering imposed by the occurrence, or the risk of occurrence of road accidents. These are considered of great importance in a Society that values human life and human welfare.
2. The more concrete and ascertainable burdens in the form of the net loss of output of goods and services due to death and injury

and the expenditure of resources necessary to make good the effects of accidents e.g. medical expenses, vehicle repairs and cost of administration.

In Reynolds's view '. . . it is beyond the competence of economists to assign objective values to the losses suffered under (category) 1 . . .' and he therefore considers only the costs in category 2, which he estimates for 1952 under the following breakdown:

(a) damage to property (e.g. damage to vehicles);
(b) medical costs (e.g. treatment of casualties);
(c) administrative costs (e.g. administration of motor insurance claims);
(d) net reduction in output (in the case of fatal accidents this is taken to be the difference between the present value of the output that the victim would have produced and the present value of his consumption if he had lived).

The total cost of damage to property due to road accidents during 1952 is estimated by extrapolating insurance company data for 1949 and inflating by the retail price index. Reynolds's estimate of this cost is £18m. (±£4m.).

Total medical costs due to road accidents during 1952 are obtained by assuming that road accidents account for 1.3 per cent of the cost of hospital services and 1.4 per cent of the cost of general medical service and the health service. The estimate for this cost is £6m. (±£2m.).

Total administrative costs due to road accidents during 1952 are estimated by assuming that half the expenditure on the administration of motor insurance is occasioned by actual accidents (rather than insurance against the possiblity of future accidents). This cost is estimated to be £12m. (±£6m.).

The net reduction in output due to road accidents during 1952 is obtained in the following manner. The average annual output *per capita* is taken to be the Net Domestic Product at factor cost divided by the number of persons in the working population. (The outputs of men and women are taken to be proportional to their respective earnings. The output of housewives is taken to be equal to the output of the average female worker.) The discounted present value of future output *per capita* is then obtained for each age group on the basis of the expected working life for that age group and the average annual output *per capita*. From the latter is subtracted the discounted present value of consumption *per capita* for the appropriate age group. Throughout, a discount rate of 4 per cent is employed. Multiplying by the numbers in each age group and adding across age groups, Reynolds estimates the total present value of loss of net output due to road deaths during 1952 as £9.5m. (±£2m.) and due to non-fatal road injuries as £26m. (±£13m.).

Finally Reynolds estimates the average cost *per casualty* as:

Death: £2000;   serious injury: £520;   slight injury: £40.

III   ABRAHAM AND THEDIÉ; 'LE PRIX D'UNE VIE HUMAINE DANS LES DECISIONS ECONOMIQUES' (1960)[1][2]

Abraham and Thedié address themselves to the question, 'How much should a society spend to save a human life?' They note the answer to such a question is to some extent dependent upon the subjective views of those who govern. They also point out that they are concerned not with the saving of life for some specific individual but rather with a reduction in the mortality rate for society.

The 'price' of an (unspecified) human life is seen as the sum of a number of elements, each element belonging to one of two broad categories: 'economic elements' and 'subjective elements'. The economic elements consist of (1) direct losses (medical treatment, damage to vehicles, burial expenditures etc.), all net of tax, and (2) losses of output. Abraham and Thedié consider three problems that arise in connection with losses of output: (i) it is necessary to decide whether to consider losses of gross or net output (the latter being output minus consumption); (ii) death has a direct demographic effect which may or may not be desirable *per se*; (iii) since losses of output in fact involve losses of future time-streams of output it is necessary for political decision-makers to specify an appropriate discount rate in order that these time-streams may be reduced to a present value.

The so called 'subjective elements' of Abraham and Thedié's price of human life consist of (1) suffering of relatives; (2) subjective costs to society (the latter arising from what to Abraham and Thedié '... semble être l'un des rôles impératifs d'une collectivité de préserver la vie de les membres'); (3) suffering of non-fatal accident victims; (4) diminution of the capacity of non-fatal accident victims to enjoy life; and finally (5) anxiety of individuals concerning the possibility of their own future involvement in accidents.

Abraham and Thedié provide no estimate for direct losses since at least part of the loss within this category depends upon the specific nature of the accident involved. However losses of gross output due to road accidents during 1957 are estimated to have an average discounted present value of 110,000 N.F. consisting of a loss of net output of 40,000 N.F. and own consumption of 70,000 N.F. A discount rate of 8 per cent is used throughout.

In deriving estimates for the subjective elements Abraham and Thedié claim no more than that they are seeking a sort of 'average opinion in society' concerning broad orders of magnitude. They argue that the best source of such information for most subjective elements is data concerning court awards. The rationale for this argument is that, the magnitude of court awards being public knowledge, judges will tend to be influenced in setting the *present* level of awards by public reaction to the size of *past* awards. In this way public opinion will tend to be reflected in the size of court awards. In terms of 1960 prices the estimates *per accident victim* are as follows:

(a) suffering of relatives: 5,000 N.F. for a bachelor, 10,000 N.F. for a married man and 20,000 N.F. for the father of a dependent family;
(b) subjective costs to society: 5,000 N.F. (Since this type of cost is clearly not considered by the courts, this is essentially Abraham and Thedié's own subjective evaluation);
(c) suffering of non-fatal accident victims: normally 1,000– 5,000 N.F. but can be as high as 5,000 N.F.;
(d) diminution of capacity of non-fatal accident victims to enjoy life: 2,000 N.F.;
(e) Anxiety: 15,000 N.F. (Like subjective costs to society, this category of cost is obviously not considered by the courts. Abraham and Thedié obtain this estimate by summing the average 'suffering of relatives' and 'subjective cost to society'.)

Abraham and Thedié conclude by noting that, while much of their argument and estimation procedure is controversial and therefore open to objection, one point seems to be irrefutable: consistent decision-making by government agencies requires *explicit* consideration of what they term the price of human life.

IV DRÈZE: 'L'UTILITÉ SOCIALE D'UNE VIE HUMAINE' (1962)[13]

Drèze conducts his analysis in two stages. In the first stage he considers the value of safety improvement from the point of view of the individual while in the second stage the valuation problem is considered in the wider context of *collective* decision-making. He argues that, provided an individual's choices under conditions of uncertainty display sufficient regularity and consistency,[14] then it is perfectly possible to use the tools of economic theory (in particular, the concepts of cardinal utility and subjective probability) to analyse the amount the individual would be willing to spend to effect various improvements in his safety.

To illustrate this point Drèze considers an individual exposed to a non-recurrent 'exceptional'[15] risk of immediate death having a (subjective) probability, p, of occurrence. The level of the individual's current wealth (net of tax) should he survive is denoted by F_v and the value of his estate (net of tax) should he die is denoted by F_m. The primary difference between F_v and F_m lies (a) in the component of human wealth which, of course, ceases to exist in the event of the individual's death, and (b) in the payoff from life insurance contracts which accrues only in the event of the individual's death. Provided that the individual's choices under uncertainty are described by the appropriate axiom system,[16] then the individual will behave as if he were an 'expected utility maximiser' so that the maximum sum, X, which he would pay to eliminate the 'exceptional' risk of immediate death, p, would be given by

$$pU_m(F_m) + (1 - p)U_v(F_v) = U_v(F_v - X) \qquad (2.1)$$

where $U_m(F_m)$ and $U_v(F_v)$ are (cardinal) utility of wealth functions contingent on life and death respectively. Drèze notes that X will increase with p at an increasing, proportional or decreasing rate as the marginal utility of wealth conditional on life is increasing, constant or decreasing. Drèze also considers the individual's decision concerning expenditure on life insurance and notes that, for the case in which the insurance premium is a proportion, π, of the sum, Y, assured, the optimal expenditure on insurance, πY, will satisfy the condition

$$\frac{d}{dY}[pU_m(F_m + Y - \pi Y) + (1 - p)U_v(F_v - \pi Y)] = 0. \qquad (2.2)$$

Drèze then proceeds to discuss the question of how much society *as a whole* should spend upon life-saving and points out that such questions involve consideration of collective decision-making and the attendant problem of external economies and costs. The latter are seen as arising either because any particular individual's death is not a matter of indifference to other individuals and/or because the probability of death for any particular individual is not independent of the probability of death for other individuals in society; i.e., to some extent safety improvements have the 'non-exclusivity' (or 'jointness') and 'non-excludability' (or non-enforceable property rights) characteristics of pure public goods.[17]

Drèze argues that *if*:

(a) individual preferences over alternative collective actions under uncertainty are representable by a cardinal utility function; and
(b) *collective* choices under uncertainty obey the same axioms as those required to ensure the existence of individual cardinal utility functions[18] (thus implying the existence of a *collective* cardinal utility function); and
(c) indifference between two collective actions on the part of every individual implies indifference in the collective ordering over actions,

then, the cardinal utility function representing the collective ordering will be such that the utility of any action under the *collective* utility function will be a weighted sum of the utilities of that action under *individual* utility functions (i.e. collective utility will be a weighted sum of individual utilities).[19] Clearly the weights reflect the relative importance placed by the collectivity on the views of each of its individual members. Given knowledge of these weights, it is then clearly possible *in principle* to proceed to an analysis of the collective valuation of safety improvements and in particular to consideration of the collective preference ordering over alternative safety-improvement schemes. What is required in addition to the weights is each *individual's* utility[20] for each alternative collective action: the weighted sum of these utilities then correctly orders the collective actions (or choices) provided that the above conditions on individual and collective choice are satisfied. Drèze offers no detailed suggestions about the manner in which the properties of individual cardinal utility functions might be established but ventures the tentative suggestion that it might be possible to infer such information from observed individual expenditures on safety improvement.

V   FROMM: 'CIVIL AVIATION EXPENDITURES' (1965)[21]

Fromm encounters the question of the value of life-saving within the wider context of an analysis designed to discover the benefits that accrue to society from government expenditures on air traffic control and airports.

After noting that the idea of placing a money value on injuries and human life is probably antithetical to the moral principles of Western society, Fromm stresses that such valuations are inevitably implicit in any allocative decision that improves or detracts from the safety of human life. ('Automobile accident fatalities, for example, would be drastically reduced ... if pedestrian crossings were ... eliminated through use of moving-belt under-passes. .... Yet such measures have not been implemented — apparently because their cost, in relation to the value of the lives they would save, appears prohibitive ...').

Fromm argues that the total loss per air carrier fatality in 1960 prices is $373,000. This figure is the aggregate of the value of the individual's life to himself, $210,000; economic loss to his family, $123,000; economic loss to the community, $4,000. Although he does not say so explicitly, Fromm would presumably regard the aggregate loss figure of $373,000 as the appropriate value of the avoidance of one airline fatality.

Unfortunately, Fromm provides very little detailed justification for these loss figures. While this omission is perhaps not so serious in the case of the various 'economic losses' whose sources are fairly obvious (see, for example, Reynolds (1956), Abraham and Thedié (1960) and Dawson (1967)), it is particularly frustrating in the altogether more problematic and contentious case of the 'value of the individual's life to himself'. However, there are indications in Fromm's paper that he regards the value to an individual of a reduction in the risk of his own death as *directly proportional* to the size of the risk reduction. Thus, if an individual would forfeit a sum x to reduce the probability of death by an amount δp, then, according to Fromm's hypothesis, the individual would pay $x/\delta p$ to avoid certain death — or, as Fromm puts it, he would value his life at $x/\delta p$.

While this does not satisfactorily explain the figure of $210,000, it does indicate a potential source: if it were possible to discover the value of small risk charges, then on Fromm's proportionality assumption this could be translated directly into a 'value of life to the individual himself'.

VI   DAWSON: *COST OF ROAD ACCIDENTS IN GREAT BRITAIN* (1967)[22] AND *CURRENT COSTS OF ROAD ACCIDENTS IN GREAT BRITAIN* (1971)[23]

Dawson's 1967 analysis is very similar in conception and execution to Reynolds's earlier work[24] and is essentially an attempt to update the latter's results by considering road accidents in Great Britain during 1963. Like Reynolds, Dawson is primarily concerned with

'. . . direct losses on which a monetary value can be placed' rather than with '. . . personal suffering and bereavement which cannot be valued directly'. Dawson does, however, discuss the nature of the so-called 'subjective costs' and in fact argues for a figure of £5000 per fatality.

Dawson is concerned to estimate '. . . the cost that could be saved as a result of a reduction in accidents' and considers categories of cost that are very similar to those employed by Reynolds. However, there are certain differences of detail. For example, Dawson values the loss of output *per capita* on the basis of average *earnings* rather than average output *per capita*. (Like Reynolds, Dawson subtracts the present value of future consumption from the present value of loss of output in the case of fatal accidents in order to compute a *net* loss of output.) Furthermore, Dawson values the output of non-working housewives at the average wage of employed women while the output *as housewives* of *working* women is valued at half the average wage rate of employed women. A further difference of detail between Reynolds's and Dawson's analysis is that, where Reynolds employs a discount rate of 4 per cent in computing present values, Dawson uses a rate of 6 per cent.

For 1963, Dawson estimates the total loss due to damage to vehicles and property as £128m.; total medical costs as £10m.; total administrative and police costs as £24m.; total net loss of output due to fatal accidents as £20m. and loss of output due to non-fatal accidents as £14m.

Dawson's estimates of the average cost *per accident* including losses of output (*net* for fatalities), medical costs, damage to property and administrative costs are: fatal accident, £3430; serious accident, £480; slight accident, £150.

Finally, Dawson considers the subjective costs imposed by road accidents. He argues that the use of court compensation awards as an estimate of the 'popular valuation' is defective for two reasons. First, the majority of court cases are concerned with more serious injuries, so that information relevant for an assessment of less serious injuries may not be available. Second, it is impossible to separate the payment made for subjective costs incurred. Dawson then briefly reviews the analysis of Abraham and Thedié[25] and finally suggests that '. . . the following rather arbitrary average values should be used for the subjective costs of casualties': fatality, £5000; serious injury, £200; slight injury, £0, the figure for a fatality being the minimum value implied by the fact that society is prepared to keep alive old-age pensioners whose contribution to net output is negative (since society is prepared to sustain an old-age pensioner whose estimated net output has a discounted present value of £5000, the value for the subjective cost of his death is clearly at least £5000).

For 1963, then, the total costs *per accident*, including subjective costs, are estimated to be: fatal accident, £8920; serious accident, £710; slight accident, £150.

In a more recent paper (Dawson (1971)), Dawson makes two major amendments to his earlier estimates of the costs of road accidents. In the first place he updates all figures to 1970 prices and in addition moves from a net to a *gross* loss of output basis for calculating the cost of output loss due to fatalities:—

The loss of output as the result of a fatal casualty in road accidents has hitherto been calculated on a net basis i.e. future production less future consumption. The argument being that when an individual was killed society lost the present value of his future output but gained by not having to provide his consumption. The problem was being looked at from the point of view of the community after the accident had happened. The reasoning now employed is based on the premise that costs are needed in order to measure the benefits arising when accidents are prevented. The accidents that need to be costed are those that do not occur but which, without the introduction of some safety measure, would have occurred. The fact that on this basis the individual concerned is, indeed, still alive means that the individual's consumption should not be deducted when assessing the benefits of preventing accidents, as he is alive and able to enjoy that consumption.

Using updated subjective costs (e.g. £5270 for a fatality) and an effective discount rate of 7 per cent (10 per cent gross discount rate *less* assumed productivity growth of 3 per cent p.a.) in place of the earlier 6 per cent, the updated estimates of average cost per accident (including the adjustment for gross losses of output in the case of fatal accidents) are: fatal accidents, £19,000; serious accidents £1400; slight accidents, £250.

Notice that all these figures are for average cost *per accident*. Since the average number of casualties per accident exceeds 1, the cost per casualty will be somewhat lower than the cost per accident (e.g. about £16,750 for a fatality). Costs per accident may be converted to approximate costs per casualty using the following data concerning average casualties per accident given in Dawson (1971):

	Class of accident		
	Fatal	Serious	Slight
Fatal casualty	1.09	—	—
Serious casualty	0.43	1.18	—
Slight casualty	0.35	0.33	1.23

VII   SCHELLING: 'THE LIFE YOU SAVE MAY BE YOUR OWN' (1968)[26]

Schelling is concerned not with placing a value upon human life *per se* but upon the *prevention of death*. Furthermore, he argues that, since it is typically not known whose deaths will be avoided by a particular safety-improvement scheme, the relevant question concerns the value that should be placed upon a reduction in the *probability* of death (which he later refers to as a reduction in 'risk') for each individual in the affected group:

It is not the worth of human life that I shall discuss, but of 'life-saving', of preventing death. And it is not a particular death but a statistical death. What is it worth to reduce the probability of death — the statistical frequency of death — within some identifiable group of people none of whom expects to die except eventually?

Schelling begins by arguing that, although death is a remote and awesome event, it is not beyond the competence of the economist to inquire about the worth of schemes designed to reduce the risk of death, especially to those whose lives are made safer. First he argues that society as a whole (including a man's immediate family and dependants) will have an interest in reducing the deleterious effects of death upon G.N.P (this is what Schelling calls the 'loss of livelihood' due to death). These effects are broadly similar to those considered and quantified by Reynolds (1956), although Schelling — more directly concerned with assessing the distribution of the burden of these costs — considers among other things the impact of a man's death upon the economic circumstances of his family, the impact upon the distribution and magnitude of the tax burden on society, and also the extent to which life insurance schemes provide an opportunity for individuals to share the financial losses occasioned by death.

However Schelling's primary contribution is to the discussion of what he calls 'consumer interest in reduced death'. He argues:

Suppose a program to save lives has been identified and we want to know its worth. The dimensions of the risks to be reduced are fairly well known, as is the reduction to be achieved. Suppose also that this risk is small to begin with, not a source of anxiety or guilt.
    Surely it is sensible to ask the question: what is it worth to the people who stand to benefit from it?

Here, Schelling stresses the value of an increase in the safety of life itself rather than the value of an increase in the safety of 'livelihood' as he calls it. However, to the extent that loss of livelihood will affect the welfare of a man's dependants after his death — and hence the aversion with which he views the prospect of his own demise — the potential loss of livelihood will not be irrelevant to 'consumer interest in reduced risk'.

Schelling argues that there are basically two ways of finding out what individuals would pay to effect a particular reduction in the risk of death. *Either* one may try to estimate the amount from information concerning preferences revealed in the market place, *or* one may *ask* people directly or indirectly. The disadvantage inherent in the first approach is, of course, that markets are subject to varying degrees of imperfection which may obfuscate underlying preferences and, furthermore, the range of marketed safety devices is limited so that one is unlikely to be able to discover much about the value of a wide spectrum of safety improvements, each offering a different degree of risk reduction. The direct inquiry approach, on the other hand, is beset with a variety of more subtle defects. How does one know that an individual's response to a direct inquiry concerning the amount he would pay to effect a particular reduction in risk is 'the truth' in the sense that it is an accurate reflection of what he *would* in fact pay if actually confronted with the option of purchasing the risk reduction? Even if the individual wished to tell the truth, how can one guarantee that he will not suffer from defective imagination in forming his response to the hypothetical choice? Will not most people be unable to comprehend the meaning of a very small risk reduction, especially if the latter is described as a very small reduction in the *probability* of death? How will the anxiety associated with the existence of the risk of death affect the individual's imaginative capacity and responses?

Schelling considers each of these problems in turn. While he acknowledges the difficulty of eliciting a 'true' response to a hypothetical question, he argues that there is no reason to suppose that the actual response will reflect 'true' preferences any less accurately than market decisions concerning expenditures on safety improvements. ('Unexpected death has a hypothetical quality whether it is merely being talked about or money is being spent to prevent it'). Both market decisions and inquiry responses suffer from the same basic problem, but Schelling sees no reason to suppose that inquiry responses suffer more. The suggested resolution to the comprehension problem associated with small changes in risk is more technical and involves the so-called 'principle of scaling of risks'.[27] This provides a means by which the amount which an individual would pay to effect a small risk change may be inferred from information concerning the value which he places on larger risk changes. That the principle should be applicable to any individual's choices requires, however, that these choices display certain fundamental regularities which may not in fact be present in decisions concerning such important potential consequences as life and death. Schelling sees the problems generated by anxiety as being closely related to the latter point. If the possible occurrence of awesome events generates anxiety, then it is probably less likely that choices among actions whose possible consequences include these events will display the kind of regularity required to justify the 'principle of scaling of risks' or, for that matter, any extrapolative estimation procedure (anxiety is probably a *discontinuous* function of risk, becoming apparent only if risk exceeds some 'threshold level'). Schelling does, however, suggest that emphasis upon explicit discussion and sophisticated analysis of risk may help to moderate the confusing impact of anxiety.

Schelling also observes that, in so far as risk reductions affect other people about whom an individual cares, it will be necessary in principle to discover the value to the individual of these reductions in other people's risk.

Finally, while Schelling is not explicit about precisely how individual valuations of risk reduction are to be used in the formation of public policy, he quite clearly considers that these values will represent 'useful information' for policy purposes so long as the policy-maker pays some heed to the principle of 'consumers' sovereignty'.

VIII   MISHAN: 'EVALUATION OF LIFE AND LIMB: A THEORETICAL APPROACH' (1971)[28]

Mishan's paper is unequivocally founded on the potential Pareto improvement view of cost—benefit analysis advocated in chapter 1 of this book. The purpose of the paper is twofold:

(a) to evaluate the consistency (with the potential Pareto improvement criterion) of existing major contributions to the literature on the value of life-saving;

(b) existing major contributions having been found to have significant deficiencies, to provide an outline of an approach to the valuation of life-saving that *is* consistent with the potential Pareto improvement criterion.

It is clear, then, that the first of Mishan's objectives is virtually identical to that pursued in this chapter.[29] Unfortunately Mishan displays a rather arbitrary selectivity in his choice of existing literature so that, while his views and arguments to some extent anticipate those propounded in Section XIII of the current chapter, it was nonetheless felt worthwhile to consider a somewhat wider range of contributions thereby providing a (hopefully) more comprehensive and more balanced critique.

Mishan suggests that, broadly speaking, four alternative methods have been advocated for placing a value on human life and hence on life-saving. The first method values a person's life in terms of the discounted present value of his expected future earnings '... exclusive of yields from ownership of non-human capital'. Mishan's objection to this method is that '... it can be rationalized only if the criterion adopted in any economic reorganization turns on the value of its contribution to G.N.P. or, more accurately, to net national product'. This particular method certainly has little if anything to do with the potential Pareto improvement criterion. Mishan then turns to the second type of approach to the valuation of life and life-saving, which involves consideration of the discounted present value of expected losses incurred by others as a consequence of someone's death. (This is essentially the conceptual foundation of Reynolds's, Dawson's and Abraham and Thedié's analyses in so far as these authors concentrate upon the losses of net output and real resource costs of accidents.) Mishan's objections to this procedure are:

(a) that it implies a positive value for the death of someone whose expected contribution to net output is negative (e.g. old age pensioners);
(b) that it ignores the feelings of the potential victims; and
(c) that it is essentially an *ex post* valuation of losses rather than an *ex-ante* valuation of *potential* losses or gains.

The third method of valuation considered by Mishan involves '... the implicit values placed on human life by the political process...'. Mishan's objection to this procedure is that, if economists are invited to provide political decision-makers with values derived from basic economic criteria of social choice, then such economists simply become involved in an empty circularity if they then refer '... a question, or part of a question received from the political process back again to the political process ...'. This valuation procedure clearly has nothing to do with the potential Pareto improvement criterion, unless by pure chance.

Unfortunately, Mishan's exposition of the fourth type of valuation procedure is rather ambiguous. He refers to this procedure as being based on 'the insurance principle' and argues that it represents an attempt '. . . to attribute a value for loss of life . . . on the implied assumption of a straight line relationship between the probability of a person being killed and the sum he would pay to cover the risk'. It is not clear, however, what Mishan means by the sum payed 'to cover the risk'. Certain parts of his argument suggest that he means the sum an individual would forfeit to eliminate the risk ('Thus if a man would pay $100 to reduce his chance of being killed by 1 per cent — say from an existing chance of one twentieth to two fiftieths — the value he places on his life is to be estimated at $10,000'), whereas in other places Mishan clearly implies that the sum payed to 'cover the risk' should be interpreted either as a premium for life insurance or as the payoff to the beneficiary under a life insurance contract: 'But even if [the linearity] assumption were both plausible and proved, the insurance principle does not yield us the required valuation. For the insurance policy makes provision in the event of a man's death only for compensation to *others*'. In so far as Mishan attributes this fourth approach to Fromm (1965), it seems reasonable to suppose that the former interpretation is intended. If this is so, then Mishan's objections (a) that the approach considers only the payoff to individuals other than the victim and (b) that it has nothing to do with the potential Pareto improvement criterion are clearly ill-founded. Mishan's only valid objection is his doubt concerning the validity of the assumption that the relationship between risk and the value of elimination of risk is linear.

Having rejected these four approaches, Mishan then proceeds to develop his own valuation procedure. In fact, Mishan provides no explicit prescription for deriving values of life-saving and accident-rate reduction, but rather develops a *taxonomy* within which such valuations may more easily proceed in a manner consistent with the potential Pareto improvement criterion. He argues that application of a cost—benefit analysis based upon the potential Pareto improvement criterion requires information concerning each affected individual's compensating variation in wealth ('. . . the maximum sum he will pay rather than forgo the project . . .') for each of the relevant categories of risk change afforded by the project. Mishan distinguishes four categories of risk:

(a) direct voluntary risks;
(b) direct involuntary risks;
(c) indirect involuntary financial risks;
(d) indirect involuntary psychic risks.

Direct voluntary risks are those '. . . that people voluntarily assume whenever they choose to buy a product or avail themselves of a service or facility' (e.g. the risks to health involved in smoking). Mishan argues that no explicit account need be taken of changes in such risk in allocative policy formation provided that consumers' compensating variations for provision of the product or service generating the direct voluntary risk enter into the policy decision, since direct voluntary risks will already be reflected in these compensating variations. ('Once the area under the demand curve [for tobacco] has been estimated and used as an approximation of the benefit smokers derive ... any further subtraction for such [direct voluntary] risks would entail double counting.')

Direct *involuntary* risks are, by contrast, those that either cannot be avoided by the individual or else cannot be avoided except at some cost. These risks are, Mishan points out, essentially in the nature of externalities and the appropriate compensating variations for changes in such risks should therefore appear *explicitly* in cost—benefit calculations.

The two categories of indirect risk are essentially associated with the death or injury of others. Indirect involuntary *financial* risks derive from the effects of the ith person's death upon the real income (or wealth) of the jth person. Similarly, indirect involuntary *psychic* risks derive from the fact that the jth person may quite simply 'care about' the ith person and therefore view with distaste the prospect of the latter's death or injury. In both cases Mishan argues that it is again necessary to take explicit account of compensating variations for changes in such risks.

Finally, Mishan, like Schelling, clearly has in mind a *probablistic* formalization of risk:

It is never the case, however, that a specific person, or a number of specific persons, can be designated in advance as being those who are certain to be killed if a specific project is undertaken. All that can be predicted, although with a high degree of confidence, is that out of a total of n members in the community an additional x members per annum will be killed. ... In the absence, therefore, of any breakdown of the circumstances surrounding the additional number of accidents to be expected, the increment of risk of being killed imposed each year on any one member of the community can be taken as x/n. ...

However, Mishan also recognises the possibility that particular individuals may over- or underestimate risks relative to the social decision-maker. It is clear, then, that Mishan is implicitly formalising risk in terms of *subjective* probabilities. For those who do over- or underestimate risks, Mishan is quite emphatic that the potential Pareto improvement criterion requires that the relevant compensating variations are those for the individual's *own* (possibly misguided) perception of the risk changes.

IX USHER: 'AN IMPUTATION TO THE MEASURE OF ECONOMIC GROWTH FOR CHANGES IN LIFE EXPECTANCY' (1973)[30]

Usher's primary objective is not to place a value on life-saving *as such*, but rather to '. . . find a natural way of combining two social indicators, the G.N.P. and mortality rates, into a single comprehensive index . . .', his basic contention being that the growth of G.N.P *alone* (failing, as it does, to take account of improvements in life expectancy) significantly understates the extent to which current generations are 'better off' than earlier generations. However, the particular procedure employed by Usher to make an imputation to the measure of economic growth for changes in life expectancy requires incidental consideration of the 'value of life' question, so that it is important to review Usher's work.

Usher assumes that individuals may be treated as 'expected utility maximisers', so that each individual may be taken to maximise U given by

$$U = \sum_{t=0}^{n} P_t U_t \qquad (2.3)$$

where P_t is the probability of survival for precisely t years, U_t is the individual's utility conditional on survival for precisely t years and n is the upper limit to the length of life. For the sake of simplicity, Usher assumes that each individual is concerned only for his own welfare so that the U_t depend solely upon the individual's anticipated time-stream of consumption, $(C_0, \ldots C_t)$. In particular, U_t is taken to have a simple, *additive-separable* form:

$$U_t = \sum_{i=0}^{t-1} \frac{C_i^{\beta}}{(1+r)^i} \qquad (2.4)$$

where β and r are utility function parameters.

Usher then defines consumption $\hat{C}(t)$ in period t *adjusted for a change in life-expectancy for some base year* $\bar{t}$ by

$$U[\hat{C}(t), D(\bar{t})] = U[C(t), D(t)] \qquad (2.5)$$

where $D(t)$ is a vector of 'age-specific' mortality rates at time t (i.e. probabilities of death during each specific period *conditional* on survival to the beginning of that period) and $C(t)$ is the *actual* consumption in period t. Notice that in view of the definition of U, $\hat{C}(t)$ is implicitly defined only for some vector of anticipated C_{t+1}, C_{t+2}, $\hat{C}_{t+1}$, $\hat{C}_{t+2}$ etc. For simplicity Usher sets $C_{t+1} = \ldots C_t$ and $\hat{C}_{t+1} = \ldots \hat{C}_t$.

It is clear, then, that $\hat{C}(t)$ defined by (2.5) is the level of consumption required in period t to compensate for the replacement of period t's 'longevity prospects' by the (typically different) prospects which prevailed in period $\bar{t}$ for an individual of the same age.

From (2.3), (2.4) and (2.5) it then follows that the rate of growth, $G_{\hat{c}}$, of $\hat{C}(t)$ is given by

$$G_{\hat{c}} = G_c + \frac{G_L}{\beta} \qquad (2.6)$$

G_c being the rate of growth of $C(t)$ and G_L the rate of growth of $L(t)$, where $L(t)$ is the value in year t of

$$\sum_{j=0}^{n} \frac{S_{j+1}}{(1+r)^j}$$

and

$$S_j = \prod_{i=0}^{j-1} (1 - D_i). \qquad (2.7)$$

Up to this point Usher's analysis is concerned with the position of a particular individual. In order to generate a value of $G_{\hat{c}}$ comparable with rates of growth of *per capita* GNP, Usher assumes that the individual analysis is applicable to *per capita* consumption and output data together with a weighted average value of G_L as if '... society were one individual writ large ...'. However, even employing these simplifications it is still necessary to estimate, among other things, a population 'average' for the utility function parameter β in order to obtain an estimate of the population $G_{\hat{c}}$. This Usher does by the following ingenious argument. He suggests first that the '... true valuation-of-life question is "How much would I pay to avoid a small probability of my death?" ' and that if a man would pay \$500 to avoid a 1-in-1000 probability of current death, then the implied value of life is \$500,000. From this it follows that the value of life for any individual is given by

$$-\frac{\partial C_0}{\partial D_0}\bigg|_U$$

i.e. 'the amount one would pay per unit for a decrease in one's mortality rate in the current year'. Again, with appropriate assumptions and definitions of consumption and mortality rates, it is possible to regard this as the appropriate expression for the population average of the value of life.

But (2.3) and (2.4) together imply that setting $C_i = C_j = C$ (for simplicity),

$$-\frac{\partial C_0}{\partial D_0}\bigg|_{i'} = \frac{C}{\beta} \sum_{j=0}^{n} \frac{S_j}{(1+r)^j} \frac{1}{(1-D_0)^2} . \qquad (2.8)$$

Thus it is possible to estimate the population 'average' for β from (2.8) given (a) assumptions about the appropriate level of C and r, (b) mortality statistics and a current age distribution and (c) population average 'value of life' appropriately defined. In seeking data concerning the latter Usher rejects estimates derived from what he calls the insurance question ('what is my life worth to my wife and children?') or the birth control question ('how much better or worse off would the community at large be if I ceased to exist or if I had never been born?'). The latter is, of course, a version of the by now familiar 'net reduction in output' considered by Reynolds, Dawson and others. Instead, Usher explicitly requires that the estimate be of $-(\partial C_0/\partial D_0)$ and regards only lines 1 and 2 of his table 1 (reproduced below as table 2.1) as relevant for this purpose, finally selecting a value of $150,000 as a basis for estimating β from the expression for $-(\partial C_0/\partial D_0)$ in equation (2.8).

X   MELINEK: 'A METHOD OF EVALUATING HUMAN LIFE FOR ECONOMIC PURPOSES' (1974)[31]

The purpose of Melinek's paper is to derive a population average of the value placed by individuals upon their own lives. No account is taken of the concern that people may have for the safety of others. The value placed upon life is defined by Melinek as '. . . the benefit [derived at the cost of accepting a given incremental risk of death] divided by the [increment in the] risk of death'. At one stage in the analysis, however, Melinek employs an estimation method (based upon the risks from smoking) which implies the subtly different definition of the value of life as the maximum amount which an individual would *forfeit* to *reduce* the risk of death by some amount, divided by the risk reduction.

Table 2-1. Scraps of evidence on the value of life
(implicit or explicit value of the life of a man about 30 years old)

	Dollars (thousands)
1. Hazard pay	
Premium miners accept for working underground	34—159
Test pilot	161
2. Medical expenditure	
Kidney transplant	72
Dialysis in hospital	270
Dialysis at home	99
3. Valuation of the cost of disease	75
4. Valuation of the cost of airplane accidents	472
5. Traffic safety	
Recommended for cost—benefit analysis by the National Safety Council	37.5
Value of life in a cost—benefit study of highways	100
6. Military decision-making	
Instructions to pilots on when to crash-land airplanes	270
Decision to produce a special ejector seat in a jet plane	4500

Melinek suggests that there are two ways of obtaining such estimates; (a) by questionnaire methods such as those outlined in Jones-Lee (1969) and (b) by direct observation of choices. While he acknowledges that the questionnaire approach has certain advantages (such as simplicity), he is doubtful of any individual's capacity to respond to hypothetical choices in a way that gives a reliable indication of how he would actually choose if confronted with a real choice. Melinek therefore opts for the direct observation approach and gives examples of three alternative possible estimation procedures.

i   Use of pedestrian subways

The essence of this approach is to discover first the critical time-saving that will induce individuals to cross a road directly rather than use a safer (but slower) subway crossing. This time differential is then taken to reflect the *minimum* benefit that would just induce people to accept the extra risk due to crossing the road so that by Melinek's definition the value of life, V_a, is given by

$$V_a = \frac{vt_c}{p_a p_d}$$

where t_c is the critical time differential, v is the marginal value of time, p_a is the probability of accident while crossing road and p_d is the probability of an accident being fatal. Using Road Research Laboratory data[32] the estimate of V_a given by this method is

$$V_a = £87,000.$$

ii   Smoking

This approach simply sets out to discover the maximum annual premium people would be prepared to pay for cigarettes that are safe but otherwise identical to ordinary cigarettes. This annual premium is then taken to be the largest aggregate amount smokers would pay to eliminate one year's deaths from smoking, the implied value of life, V_b, being given by the premium per death avoided. Using Fire Research Station data, Central Statistical Office data and Royal College of Physicians data,[33] and deflating the number of deaths avoided to take account of the typical time lag between death and the smoking responsible for death, V_b is estimated to be

$$V_b = £28,000.$$

iii   Employment

This approach is designed to elicit a value of life from the wage premia for risky occupations.[34] Using Central Statistical Office data[35] on industrial accidents and International Labour Office (ILO) data[36] on job evaluation, the value of life V_c is estimated to be

$$V_c = £200,000.$$

It should be noted that this method rests upon a rather obscure and precarious argument concerning the relationship between the standard deviation of the ILO job evaluation points distribution and the standard deviation of the wage rate distribution, so that it is not at all clear that Melinek has in fact measured the appropriate wage rate premia.

XI   AKEHURST AND CULYER: 'ON THE ECONOMIC SURPLUS AND THE VALUE OF LIFE' (1974)[37]

Akehurst and Culyer begin by expressing their agreement with the general methodology propounded by Mishan (1971). However, they doubt the current applicability — except at high cost — of any valuation procedures consistent with Mishan's methodology[38] and in consequence propose their own procedure for valuing increases in human longevity. Paradoxically, the Akehurst and Culyer method, which its authors claim is consistent with Mishan's methodology, is also closely related to the 'earned income' approach[39] criticised by Mishan as being relevant to a G.N.P — maximisation criterion rather than the potential Pareto improvement criterion.

Specifically, Akehurst and Culyer propose that the value of an increment in longevity be taken to be the discounted present value of *half* of the income earned as a consequence of the prolongation of life, with adjustments for transfer payments and other factors. Akehurst and Culyer advocate this particular measure because they regard the non-existence of an opportunity to work as 'economic' death and one-half of earnings approximates the surplus — or compensating variation — for being able to trade leisure for income (i.e. for being able to work) over the increment of life. As they put it,

. . . a major benefit to an individual from prolongation of life evidently lies to a degree in his increased wealth from prolonged earning time. This has been recognised in the literature, though the full significance of the qualification 'to a degree' has not been appreciated. It is reasonable to argue that a minimum estimate of the economic surplus a man gains from being alive is the surplus he gains from being able to work. The conceptually correct measure is not, however, the amount earned, but the economic surplus from working.

Finally, Akehurst and Culyer note that on the usual assumptions about the individual supply curve for labour, 'the proposed approximation will be smaller than the true surplus at all wage rates. It consequently has two major advantages: it is extremely simple to calculate and it has a (qualitatively) known relationship with the conceptually correct measure.'

XII   GHOSH, LEES AND SEAL: 'OPTIMAL MOTORWAY SPEED AND SOME VALUATIONS OF TIME AND LIFE' (1975)[40]

Ghosh, Lees and Seal's basic premise is that at the socially optimal average speed on a motorway the marginal social benefit from increased speed (in the form of time-saving) will just equal the marginal social cost (in the form of increased fuel consumption and increased casualty rates).

From this proposition, together with a definitional speed—time-saving relationship, a speed—fuel-consumption relationship and a speed—casualty relationship (the latter two relationships estimated from recent data[41]), it is then possible to express the optimal average motorway speed as a function of, among other things,

(a) the total traffic volume in miles per month;
(b) a value of time;
(c) the price of fuel;
(d) an average cost per casualty.

Ghosh, Lees and Seal then perform a number of conceptual experiments using this basic expression for the optimal average motorway speed. For example, employing a cost per casualty figure of £2445.34 derived from Dawson's (1971) paper (basically this is a weighted average of Dawson's costs of fatal, serious and slight injuries, the weights being the appropriate historical proportions of each type of casualty) together with a fuel price of £0.35 per gallon, Ghosh, Lees and Seal obtain the following optimal average speeds corresponding to various alternative values of time:

£1.00/hr: 67.45 mph
£0.50/hr: 47.69 mph
£0.25/hr: 33.72 mph

It is also shown that a doubling of the cost per casualty has a very small impact on the optimal average speed (e.g. for a value of time of £1.00/hr, the optimal average speed falls to 62.30 mph).

In another such experiment it is assumed that the *actual* average motorway speed for the period under analysis (58.8 mph) was in fact *optimal*. A value of time of £1.00/hr and a price of petrol of £0.35 per gallon are then shown to imply a value of life (the cost of a motorway fatality) of £94,000. However, this figure is highly sensitive to the assumed value of time and price of petrol, being an increasing function of the value of time and a decreasing function of the price of petrol. (For example, the authors point out that if the value of time is reduced to £0.63/hr with the price of petrol and optimal speed constant, the implied value of life falls to *zero*. Similarly, in an earlier version of their paper they showed that if the price of petrol is reduced to zero with the value of time and optimal speed constant, the value of life rises to £252,260.)

XIII   A CRITIQUE OF EXISTING ANALYSES

In chapter 1 it was argued that in order to conduct a cost—benefit analysis for a particular allocative adjustment it is necessary to establish the size and sign of the relevant compensating variations in wealth. It was also argued that the ease with which these compensating variations may be estimated depends crucially upon whether or not there exist markets for the commodities whose aggregate output and distribution are affected by the allocative adjustment under consideration. If the relevant commodities *are* exchanged in markets, then it will usually be possible to utilise information concerning market demand and supply functions to estimate compensating variations. If, however, the relevant commodities are *not* exchanged in markets (e.g. externalities and public goods) then the difficulties involved in estimating compensating variations are rather more severe.

Clearly there do exist markets for certain types of safety-improvement devices (e.g. seat belts and motorcycle crash helmets). However, it is almost certainly true that the vast majority of safety-improvement devices are non-marketed public goods — safe roads, once constructed, indiscriminately tend to make life safer for all who travel on them. Now markets for the restricted range of safety-improvement devices that are also genuine private goods will provide information *only* about compensating variations for the degrees of safety improvement afforded by these devices. Since it is unlikely that public investment programmes will affect safety in precisely the same degree as marketed commodities designed to improve safety, information derived from these markets will be of very limited use for cost—benefit analysis.

How, then, is one to proceed? Clearly a potentially fruitful first step is simply to list the possible effects of an improvement in safety for any subset of the population. Let us therefore consider some hypothetical safety improvement that is expected to reduce the fatality rate by s (unspecified) lives in a population of N people, and let us for simplicity assume that this safety improvement will be effective only during a single time period — say, one year. (Safety improvements that reduce the number of non-fatal accidents will be considered at a later stage.)

This anticipated reduction in the fatality rate will have three primary effects. In the first place it will reduce the real resource cost borne by society due to damage to physical capital (e.g. vehicles and roads) and will also reduce the input of medical, administrative and legal resources inevitably involved in the aftermath of a death. The second effect of the anticipated reduction in the mortality rate derives from the possibility that an individual's lifetime consumption — discounted in some appropriate way to a present value — may be less than the present value of his contribution to national output. That is, the individual may make a *net* contribution to output. If this is the case then the rest of society benefits from the net contribution to output (or 'net output') in a manner determined by the distribution of income in the society. Clearly, part of this net output is extinguished by the individual's premature demise so that one way in which a reduction in the fatality rate benefits society is by reducing the amount of net output extinguished by premature death.[42] The third (and, almost certainly, most important[43]) effect of a reduction in the fatality rate is quite simply that, during the relevant time period, it diminishes the likelihood of death for any particular person (or anyone he cares about). More formally, in the case of the hypothetical anticipated reduction in the fatality rate by s unspecified lives in a population of N people, we can say that life will be made 'safer' for everyone in the relevant population in the particular sense that the *probability* of death for any specific individual is diminished during the period of time for which the fatality rate is reduced. In certain rare cases it may be known precisely *whose* lives will be saved by a particular safety improvement. Such cases may be described in the current context by saying that the reduction in the probability of death for such individuals is unity while the reduction for all other individuals is zero.

This immediately raises the question of what is meant by 'probability' in this context. Since this question will be discussed at considerable length in later chapters, suffice it to say at this stage that probability is to be treated merely as a formalisation of an individual's subjective 'degree of belief' that a particular event will occur. All that is being suggested is that a reduction in the fatality rate by s (unspecified) lives in a population of N individuals will cause each individual to reduce his degree of belief in the occurrence of his own death during the relevant period of time. Furthermore each individual will presumably also revise his degree of belief in those events involving the death of anyone he cares about.

Before proceeding to consider the means by which the compensating variations for each of these three effects might be estimated, it is important to be clear about the fundamental differences between the third effect and the first two. An individual will value the prospect of a safety improvement for two basic reasons. In the first place an anticipated reduction in the fatality rate will reduce the real resource and output losses that can be expected to be occasioned by the death of other people. The first two aspects reflect this point. However, an individual will *also* value a safety improvement because it reduces the likelihood of occurrence — to himself or anyone else he cares about — of an extremely undesirable event. The third effect reflects the latter point. In essence, the distinction between the third effect and the first two is that the latter arise because human beings are averse to the *consequences* of the death of other people, whereas the former arises because human beings are averse to death *per se*.

Let us now consider the compensating variations associated with (a) the anticipated reduction in real resource costs, (b) the anticipated avoidance of loss of net output and (c) the anticipated reduction in the probability of death.

The compensating variations in category (a) are relatively easy to deal with. The real resource costs associated with death will be distributed among the members of society in some manner determined by the distribution of wealth and the nature of the tax system. Provided that individuals correctly anticipate their share of total real resource costs, then they will in aggregate be prepared to forfeit precisely δR in order to reduce total real resource costs by an amount δR.[44] The aggregate compensating variation in category (b) is, by a similar argument, precisely equal to the value of net output that will be produced by those whose premature deaths will be avoided by the reduction in the fatality rate. Again, the distribution of this extra net output will be determined by the distribution of net-of-tax income, so that if individuals correctly anticipate their shares of the incremental net output, they will be prepared to pay in aggregate an amount precisely equal to its value in order to avoid its loss. There is, however, one fairly serious difficulty associated with estimation of compensating variations for avoidance of reduction in net output. Since it is typically not known whose premature deaths will be avoided by a reduction in the fatality rate, then it is not known by precisely how much net output will be affected. Clearly the relevant compensating variation is the *certainty equivalent* of the essentially uncertain gain in net output.

The compensating variations in category (c) are altogether more problematic than those in the previous two categories. It is the central contention of this book that information concerning these compensating variations can be obtained only by inquiring into the nature of individuals' basic attitudes to risk-taking and that a foundation for such an inquiry is provided by the theory of choice under uncertainty developed by Ramsey,[45] Von Neumann and Morgenstern,[46] Savage[47] and others. However, since these matters will be considered at length in later chapters they will not be discussed further at this stage.

So far the discussion has been solely concerned with anticipated reductions in the number of *fatal* accidents. Most of what has been said, however, applies with slight modification to safety improvements that are expected to affect the *non-fatal* accident rate. The only important difference is that, since a non-fatal accident victim's future consumption is not extinguished, involvement in a non-fatal accident implies an unequivocal loss of output for society during the period in which the victim's output is impaired. (It will be recalled that in the case of fatal accidents the victim's future consumption is extinguished so that society suffers a *net* loss of output *only if* the present value of lost output exceeds the present value of extinguished consumption.)

We are now in a position to consider the extent to which each of the analyses summarised in sections I to XII contributes to an understanding of the nature and magnitude of the compensating variations discussed above. A natural starting point is Dawson (1971), since he is the only author to advocate use of a *gross* loss of output measure for the cost of a fatal accident, suggesting that, since the individual concerned is '... still alive ... the individual's consumption should not be deducted when assessing the benefits of preventing accidents, as he is alive and able to enjoy that consumption'. This view is coherent only if the object of economic policy is G.N.P maximisation, which, as already noted in section VIII, has little, if anything, to do with the potential Pareto improvement criterion.

The paper by Ghosh, Lees and Seal is also unique in its approach to the problem of the value of life. In so far as the authors are concerned to estimate such a value — and this is by no means the sole purpose of their paper — the approach employed is to *suppose* that current average motorway speeds are socially optimal and to infer the implied value of life from a time-saving/fuel-cost/safety tradeoff. While it must be conceded that this is a most ingenious method of eliciting the value of life implied by one important aspect of the social arrangement, it would nonetheless seem that, for the purposes of estimating the aggregate compensating variation for a safety improvement, this approach suffers from precisely those limitations noted by Mishan in his discussion of the use of '... implicit values placed on human life by the political process ...' (see section VIII above).

Dublin and Lotka, Reynolds and Dawson (1967) are clearly almost exclusively concerned with what we have called 'real resource costs' and 'losses of net output', as are Abraham and Thedié, who also devote a substantial portion of their paper to discussion of these categories of loss. What these analyses do not do, however, is to offer any discussion of the compensating variations associated with improvements in individual safety *per se*. Both Reynolds and Dawson recognise the existence of essentially subjective costs of accidents and death. However, Reynolds simply eschews detailed consideration of these costs while Dawson's analysis of this element of the problem is superficial to say the least, providing at best only a lower bound to the appropriate value. Abraham and Thedié discuss what they call the 'subjective elements' of the price of human life, but their valuation of these subjective elements is based either upon the magnitude of court awards or, for certain categories of subjective cost, upon their own subjective valuation. Clearly, since neither procedure is related in any satisfactory manner to the notion of an aggregate-compensating variation for a change in the probability of death, Abraham and Thedié's estimation of the subjective elements of the price of human life must be counted irrelevant to the current problem.

In fact, the fundamental deficiency of Reynolds's, Dawson's and Abraham and Thedié's analyses is that they are all essentially concerned with the concept of a 'cost per accident'. This inevitably leads to the philosophically and economically intractable concept of a 'subjective cost' per accident or (worse still) the 'subjective cost of death'. Had these writers approached the problem by asking the kind of question most pertinent to cost—benefit analysis (i.e. 'do those who gain by the safety improvement do so by a sufficient amount to compensate those who lose?'), *and* had they also recognised that the relevant gain — apart from avoidance of real resource costs and net output losses — is typically a small reduction in the risk of one's own death or the death of those one cares about, then they would have avoided the sterile, confusing and contentious problems posed by the 'subjective costs' of death and non-fatal accidents.

Fromm's contribution is in some respects similar to those already discussed. For example, he considers the various costs of death under categories that broadly resemble those adopted by Abraham and Thedié. Where his contribution differs, however, is in his treatment of the 'value of an individual's life to himself'. Fromm is clearly aware of the importance of the idea of the value of a change in the *probability* of death, arguing that this value, v, will be a simple linear function of the probability change, δp, i.e.

$$v = k\delta p. \qquad (2.9)$$

This provides a means of relating the value of a change in the probability of death to an individual's valuation of his own life (which Fromm takes to be the value of avoiding certain death). Setting $\delta p = 1$ in equation (2.9) gives the value of avoiding certain death as k. Clearly, if Fromm's assumption concerning the relationship between v and δp is correct then this provides a simple and potentially appealing bridge between the idea of the value of a change in risk and the concept of the value of life. Unfortunately, as will be shown in chapter 5, Fromm's hypothesis is at the very least open to doubt.

The papers by Akehurst and Culyer and Drèze contrast with those already discussed in concentrating upon the *subjective* aspects of the value of life and safety improvement rather than the real resource costs and net output losses associated with accidents and death. Akehurst and Culyer argue that a lower bound to the value placed by an individual on an investment in longevity is given by his compensating variation (or 'surplus') from being able to work over the increased period of life. There are at least two objections to this measure. In the first place it bears no relation to an individual's valuation of a *small change* in the risk of death which, it was argued earlier, appears to be the relevant notion for most cost—benefit analyses of safety improvement in view of the fact that it is typically not known specifically whose lives will be saved. However, suppose that it *was* known precisely whose lives were to be saved by a particular safety improvement. Even under these circumstances there remains a further objection to Akehurst and Culyer's measure. If failure to work implies death (presumably by starvation), then the compensating variation for being able to work at the *subsistence wage* during the period of increased longevity would give the value of living over this period. However, the compensating variation for being able to work at any higher wage rate will clearly give an *overestimate* of this value. Since it will presumably be the case that most people earn a wage well above the subsistence level, it is clear that Akehurst and Culyer's measure will overestimate the value of living if failure to work implies death. If, on the other hand, the individual does not expect that he would die should he fail to work, then the compensating variation for being able to work will be unrelated to the value of living. For these reasons, then, it would appear that the Akehurst—Culyer measure has little relevance for the kind of cost—benefit analysis under discussion in this book.

In contrast, the paper by Drèze is without doubt one of the most important contributions to the literature on the value of safety.

Drèze quite explicitly approaches the problem from the point of view of changes in the *probability* of death and individual decision-making under uncertainty. However, he does not employ his analytical framework to consider the nature and magnitude of compensating variations. None the less, his paper does provide a foundation upon which such an analysis can be built and chapter 5 of this book owes much to Drèze's ideas.

Schelling and Mishan are primarily concerned with the overall methodology of public decision-making in the sphere of safety improvement rather than with the detailed development of procedures for eliciting qualitative and quantitative information concerning the value of safety. In general one can find little to quarrel with in the overall approach advocated in these papers since both authors appear to view the problem in much the same way as this book suggests it ought to be viewed. However, Mishan's paper would seem to deserve criticism on two counts, both associated with his critique of the existing literature. In the first place he omits to mention certain papers that make substantial contributions *along the general lines that he himself advocates*, notable among these omissions being the paper by Drèze. The second objection to Mishan's paper is more minor and is concerned with his criticism of the 'net output' approach on the grounds that it is an *ex-post* valuation, the relevant concept being in Mishan's view an *ex-ante* measure. While one would not deny the latter point, Mishan's criticism is ill-founded if (as assumed in this book) individuals correctly anticipate the gains in net output, since under these circumstances the *ex-post* and *ex-ante* values are identical.

From the point of view of basic methodology, both Schelling and Mishan argue that potential changes in fatality and accident rates are most fruitfully viewed as changes in the *probability* of death or injury and that what is important for public decision-making is the value that individuals *themselves* place upon these changes in probability. Mishan does not discuss the manner in which these values might be estimated but Schelling provides a few tentative suggestions concerning possible experimental procedures. The latter would, however, need considerable refinement and modification before they could be expected to form the basis for any workable estimation procedure. One of the problems associated with Schelling's suggested experimental procedure is that it lacks an adequate foundation in the theory of choice under uncertainty, and this has the added disadvantage that the analysis provides no substantial insights of a purely qualitative nature. Of course Schelling was almost certainly concerned merely to advocate systematic inquiry into the values placed by individuals upon changes in safety and in this objective his paper should surely be judged to succeed.

Finally, Usher and Melinek both attempt to apply the general methodology advocated by Schelling and Mishan, concentrating upon individuals' valuation of changes in their own safety rather than upon changes in the safety of others or upon avoidance of real resource costs or losses of net output. Usher's contribution is largely qualitative and theoretical, his empirical material being merely a summary of other work, while Melinek's is primarily empirical, having little if any theoretical foundation. Judged as a contribution to the theoretical analysis of the value of safety, Usher's work suffers from a number of rather serious limitations. In the first place he considers only an individual's concern for his *own* safety and in addition fails to consider the important part played by life insurance in allowing a redistribution of wealth between the contingencies of survival and demise. The other limitations of Usher's model arise largely from the particularly restrictive additive-separable form that he assumes for the conditional utility function defined on time-streams of consumption (see equation (2.4) above). Among other things, this implies that for parameter values within the range allowed by Usher it is possible to make the individual *indifferent* to the length of time for which he survives, his concern being only with the discounted present value of his consumption during the period for which he does survive. Usher also concentrates his attention upon the individual's marginal rate of substitution between *current* consumption and the age-specific mortality rate for the current period, referring to this as the 'value of life',[48] whereas the more appropriate concept in the context of a conventional cost—benefit analysis (concerned with aggregate-compensating variations in wealth) would seem to be the marginal rate of substitution between *wealth* and the appropriate mortality rate. Despite these and other problems, Usher's paper is a most interesting attempt to develop a theoretical framework for the analysis of changes in safety along the general lines advocated by Schelling and Mishan. It is perhaps because Usher is concerned largely with other matters (such as the imputation to the rate of growth for improvements in life expectancy) that he is prepared to work with a less-than-ideally general analytical apparatus.

Melinek, in contrast to Usher, concentrates almost exclusively upon the empirical estimation of a value of life which, despite Melinek's failure to make the point explicitly, amounts to an essentially marginal rate of substitution between wealth and risk.[49]

The major objection to Melinek's analysis — apart from its lack of an explicit theoretical foundation — is that it embodies no attempt to test the proposition upon which the entire exercise is premised, namely that the observed premia for risky occupations or the minimum acceptable time savings on a road crossing are in fact due solely to the increments in risk involved. Furthermore, in converting these premia to a rate of substitution it is necessary to divide by the appropriate increment in risk. But what is the appropriate increment? Is it, as Melinek assumes, the increment perceived by the social decision-maker or technical expert appraising the variation in risk, or is it the increment perceived by the individual? This question is particularly important in view of the fact that for various reasons the two perceptions may be radically different.

In summary, the work of Dublin and Lotka, Reynolds, Dawson, Abraham and Thedié bears only upon the estimation of aggregate-compensating variations for the avoidance of real resource costs and losses of net output. It is therefore relevant only for a limited aspect of the problem in hand. In order to consider the more perplexing (and, one suspects, quantitatively more important) problem of aggregate-compensating variations for individual safety improvement *per se*, what is required is an analysis founded in the philosophical position advocated by Schelling and Mishan and developed from the analytical framework provided by Drèze. In certain respects the work of Usher and Melinek represents an attempt to evolve this type of analysis, but for reasons outlined above both of these stimulating papers suffer from important theoretical and/or empirical limitations. The remainder of this book is therefore devoted to the development of what is hopefully a comprehensive qualitative and quantitative analysis free from at least some of these limitations.

NOTES

1. Dublin and Lotka (1930). A revised edition published in 1946 presents substantially similar arguments but employs more recent data.
2. The 'age-specific' mortality rate for an individual aged x is simply the proportion of individuals surviving to age x who then die during their $x + 1$st year. It is therefore essentially the *probability* of death during the $x + 1$st year *conditional* on survival to age x.
3. This is an average in the sense that it is one-hundred thousandth of the *total* present value of net earnings for a population of one hundred thousand people, a proportion of whom die at age x, others at age y, others at age z and so on, the proportions being taken from a standard mortality table. (See

the appendix to chapter 5 for a discussion of the contents of standard mortality tables.)

4. Petty (1699) p. 192.
5. Farr (1876).
6. Lüdtke (1873) p. 513.
7. Smith (1786).
8. Engel (1883).
9. Nicholson (1896).
10. Marshall (1920) Book VI, Chapter IV.
11. Reynolds (1956).
12. Abraham and Thedié (1960).
13. Drèze (1962).
14. That is, provided the individual's choices under uncertainty obey a version of the Von Neumann—Morgenstern or Savage axioms (see Von Neumann and Morgenstern (1953) and Savage (1954)) *modified* to accommodate (a) the existence of a preference ordering over the various 'states of the world', which determine the consequences of each alternative action open to the individual, and (b) the possibility that the subjective probabilities associated with alternative states of the world may *not* be parametric. For a full discussion of the nature and implications of such an axiom system see, for example, Luce and Krantz (1971).
15. An 'exceptional' risk is defined by Drèze as a non-recurrent risk of immediate death in excess of the normal level.
16. See n. 14 above.
17. For a discussion of the nature and properties of public goods see for example Head (1962).
18. See, for example, Savage (1954).
19. For a more detailed discussion of this proposition see Harsanyi (1955).
20. Strictly these will be the *expected* utilities associated with each action.
21. Fromm (1965).
22. Dawson (1967).
23. Dawson (1971).
24. Reynolds (1956).
25. Abraham and Thedié (1960).
26. Schelling (1968).
27. Suppose that an individual is indifferent between consequence A with certainty and a gamble involving a probability p_1 of consequence B and a probability $(1 - p_1)$ of consequence C. The principle of scaling of risks asserts that the individual would then be indifferent between on the one hand a gamble involving a probability of p_2 of consequence A and a probability $(1 - p_2)$ of consequence C and on the other hand a gamble involving a probability $p_1 p_2$ of consequence B and a probability $(1 - p_1 p_2)$ of consequence C.
28. Mishan (1971).
29. In fact, the author's doctoral thesis, submitted before Mishan's paper was published, contains an argument similar in spirit, if not in detail, to Mishan's.

30. Usher (1973).
31. Melinek (1974).
32. Road Research Laboratory (1963).
33. Melinek, Woolley and Baldwin (1973), Central Statistical Office (1972) and Royal College of Physicians (1971).
34. As far as the author is aware, there are at least two other studies in progress (or as yet unpublished) concerning wage premia for risky occupations. The first by Thaler and Rosen (see Thaler and Rosen (1973)) estimates the equilibrium marginal rate of substitution between income and risk (which is tantamount to a 'value of life' — see n. 48 below) to be about $200,000 for risk changes effective over a period of one year. The second study, currently being conducted by Needleman, is concerned not merely with estimation of individuals' valuation of their *own* safety from risky wage premia, but also with an attempt to estimate the value placed on improvements in the safety of close relatives from data concerning kidney transplants.
35. Central Statistical Office (1968, 1972).
36. International Labour Office (1960).
37. Akehurst and Culyer (1974).
38. In particular, Akehurst and Culyer discuss the method proposed by the author (see Jones-Lee (1969)).
39. See section VIII above.
40. Ghosh, Lees and Seal (1975).
41. The speed—fuel consumption relationship is taken from the Department of the Environment (1972), while the speed—casualty relationship is estimated using monthly data for the period January 1972—March 1974.
42. Of course, it is possible that for some people the present value of future consumption *exceeds* the present value of future output (e.g. individuals past retirement age). In such cases premature death benefits the rest of society to the extent that it increases its share of GNP. This is *not* to say that society would *wish* such individuals to die — other effects of death will almost certainly be regarded as so undesirable as to far outweigh the increased share of GNP for the rest of society.
43. This assertion seems to need little defence except in the case of suicides or misanthropes and even these may have a marked, if perverse, interest in personal safety.
44. Denote the ith individual's share of total real resource costs by $f_i(R)$ so that $\Sigma_i f_i(R) = R$. If the reduction in total real resource costs is δR then, provided he correctly anticipates his share of the reduction, the ith individual's compensating variation is given by $f_i(R) - f_i(R - \delta R)$ so that the aggregate compensating variation is given by $\Sigma_i \{f_i(R) - f_i(R - \delta R)\} = \delta R$.
45. Ramsey (1931).
46. Von Neumann and Morgenstern (1953).
47. Savage (1954).
48. See chapter 5, section IX for a discussion of the relationship between marginal valuations of changes in the risk of death and the 'value of life'.
49. See n. 48.

REFERENCES

Abraham, C. and Thedié, J. 'Le Prix d'une Vie Humaine dans Les Decisions Economiques' *Revue Française de Recherche Opérationelle* (1960)

Akehurst, R. and Culyer, A. J. 'On the Economic Surplus and the Value of Life' *Bulletin of Economic Research* (November 1974)

Central Statistical Office, *Annual Abstract of Statistics* No. 105, London, HMSO (1968)

Central Statistical Office, *Annual Abstract of Statistics* No. 109, London, HMSO (1972)

Dawson, R. F. F. *Cost of Road Accidents in Great Britain* London, Road Research Laboratory, Ministry of Transport (1967)

Dawson, R. F. F. *Current Costs of Road Accidents in Great Britain* London, Road Research Laboratory, Department of the Environment (1971)

Department of the Environment, *Getting the Best Roads for our Money: The COBA Method of Appraisal* London, HMSO (1972)

Drèze, J. 'L'Utilité Sociale d'une Vie Humaine' *Revue Française de Recherche Opérationelle* (1962)

Dublin, L. I. and Lotka, A. J. *The Money Value of a Man* New York, Ronald Press (1930)

Engel, E. 'Der Werth des Menschen' in *Volkswirtshafliche Zeitfragen* (1883)

Farr, W. *Contribution to 39th Annual Report of the Registrar General of Births, Marriages and Deaths for England and Wales (1876)*

Fromm, G. 'Civil Aviation Expenditures' in Dorfman, R. (ed.) *Measuring Benefits of Government Investments* Washington, Brookings (1965)

Ghosh, D., Lees, D. and Seal, W. 'Optimal Motorway Speed and Some Valuations of Time and Life' *Manchester School* (June 1975)

Harsanyi, J. 'Cardinal Welfare, Individualistic Ethics and Interpersonal Comparisons of Utility' *Journal of Political Economy* (1955)

Head, J. G. 'Public Goods and Public Policy' *Public Finance* (1962)

International Labour Office *Job Evaluation Studies and Reports New Series* No. 56, Geneva (1960)

Jones-Lee, M. W. 'Valuation of Reduction in Probability of Death by Road Accident' *Journal of Transport Economics and Policy* (January 1969)

Luce, R. D. and Krantz, D. H. 'Conditional Expected Utility' *Econometrica* (March 1971)

Lüdtke, R. Contribution to *Deutsche Verisicherungs-Zeitung* (1873)

Marshall, A. *Principles of Economics* London, Macmillan (1920)

Melinek, S. J. 'A Method of Evaluating Human Life for Economic Purposes' *Accident Analysis and Prevention* (October 1974)

Melinek, S. J., Woolley, S. K. D. and Baldwin, R. *Analysis of a Questionnaire on Attitudes to Risk* Borehamwood Joint Fire Research Organization Fire Research Note No. 962 (1973)

Mishan, E. J. 'Evaluation of Life and Limb: A Theoretical Approach' *Journal of Political Economy* (July/August 1971)

Nicholson, J. S. *Strikes and Social Problems* London, Macmillan (1896)

Von Neumann, J. and Morgenstern, O. *Theory of Games and Economic Behavior* Princeton University Press (1953)

Petty, W. *Political Arithmetick, or a Discourse Concerning the Extent and Value of Lands, People, Buildings etc.* London, Robert Clavel (1699)

Ramsey, F. P. *The Foundations of Mathematics and Other Logical Essays* New York, Harcourt Brace (1931)

Reynolds, D. J. 'The Cost of Road Accidents' *Journal of the Royal Statistical Society* (1956)

Road Research Laboratory, *Research on Road Safety* London, HMSO (1963)

Royal College of Physicians, *Smoking and Health* London, Pitman (1971)

Savage, L. J. *The Foundations of Statistics* New York, Wiley (1954)

Schelling, T. C. 'The Life You Save May Be Your Own', in Chase, S. B. (ed.) *Problems in Public Expenditure Analysis* Washington, Brookings (1968)

Smith, A. *Wealth of Nations*, 4th edn, London, Strahan and Cadell (1786)

Thaler, R. and Rosen, S. 'The Value of Saving a Life: Evidence from the Labour Market' *University of Rochester Graduate School of Management Working Paper* no. 7401 (December 1973)

Usher, D. 'An Imputation to the Measure of Economic Growth for Changes in Life Expectancy' in *NBER Conference on Research in Income and Wealth* (1973)

3. Choice under Uncertainty[1]

In chapter 2 it was argued that the *ex-ante* anonymity of those whose death or injury will be avoided by a reduction in the fatal or non-fatal accident rate means that a primary effect of such reductions is a (typically small) decrease in the *risk* of death or injury. From the discussion in chapters 1 and 2 it is clear, then, that an important prerequisite for a cost—benefit analysis of safety improvements is information concerning the aggregate-compensating variation for these small decreases in risk. That is, we must inquire — first at the individual and then at the aggregate level — into the relationship between the magnitude of a decrease in risk and the maximum amount that would be paid[2] to affect that change. *Thus stated, the problem is clearly one of choice under uncertainty.* The present chapter is therefore devoted to a brief exposition of that branch of the theory of choice (or decision-making) under uncertainty which will form the foundation for later chapters' analysis of compensating variations for changes in the risk[3] of death or injury.

A glossary of the notation employed in this chapter appears on pages 68 and 69.

I STATES OF THE WORLD AND DEGREES OF BELIEF

The most general description that can be given of a situation involving choice under uncertainty is based upon the concept of a set of mutually exclusive 'states of the world'. In essence, a state of the world is a description of the world sufficiently complete that the decision-maker is able to associate with each of his alternative actions (or decisions) a determinate consequence contingent upon occurrence of that state of the world. That is, if the decision-maker knew which state of the world would occur, then he would anticipate with *certainty* the consequence of each of his alternative actions. A decision-making situation under uncertainty is then characterised by the existence of *more than one* possible state of the world and *more than one* possible action, at least one action having consequences that are not identical in all states of the world.

Clearly, what constitutes a relevant partition of world descriptions into mutually exclusive states of the world depends upon the decision-making situation under analysis. For the decision concerning whether or not to accept a bet on the outcome of the toss of a coin there are only *two* relevant states — 'heads' and 'tails'. For a businessman planning the scale and nature of a new factory, the number of relevant states will clearly be very much larger, and in addition each state will necessarily involve an extremely exhaustive world description including, for example, specification of the outcome of current research programmes, the outcome of the next general election, rivals' actions, etc.

Suppose that in some situation an individual must choose one of *m* alternative actions, a_i $(i = 1 \ldots m)$, and that there are *n* relevant mutually exclusive states of the world, s_j $(j = 1 \ldots n)$. The decision problem confronting the individual may then be described by an $m \times n$ array of contingent consequences, c_{ij}, the latter being complete descriptions of the consequences uniquely determined by actions and states of the world:

	s_1	s_2	s_3			s_n
a_1	c_{11}	c_{12}	c_{13}	.	. .	—
a_2	c_{21}	c_{22}	c_{23}	.	. .	—
a_3	c_{31}	c_{32}	c_{33}	.	. .	—
.	.	.	.	.	. .	.
.	.	.	.	.	. .	.
.	.	.	.	.	. .	.
a_m	—	—	—	.	. .	c_{mn}

Furthermore, the *i*th action is *completely described* by the *i*th row of this array, so that we can identify actions with *n*-tuples of contingent consequences:[4]

$$a_i = (c_{i1}, c_{i2}, \ldots c_{in}). \qquad (3.1)$$

It will frequently, though by no means always, be the case that the c_{ij} will be levels of wealth, or income or profit. In such cases the decision problem is described by a real *matrix* $[c_{ij}]$ while the *i*th action may be viewed as a $1 \times n$ *vector* of reals.

It is probably fair to say that the most fundamental disagreement among those seeking to analyse the problem of choice under uncertainty concerns the appropriate procedure for formally describing the extent of a decision-maker's confidence (or 'degree of belief') in the occurrence of each state of the world. In essence there are four approaches to this problem:

(a) to formalise degrees of belief as *objective* probabilities;
(b) to formalise degrees of belief as *subjective* probabilities;
(c) to formalise degrees of belief in terms of 'degrees of potential surprise';
(d) to give no *explicit* formalisation of degrees of belief.

From the point of view of pure mathematics, probability is simply a measure defined on the class, $\mathscr{C}$, of subsets of a sample space, S. To be more explicit, the development of the mathematical theory of probability starts with the undefined primitive concept of a *simple event*. The *sample space*, S, is defined as the set of all simple events, subsets of the sample space being known as *events*. The *probability* of any event, E, is then defined as the image of that event under a function P from $\mathscr{C}$ (the class of events) on to the closed interval $[0, 1]$ on the real line. The function P is required to satisfy two conditions, the first being

$$P(S) = 1. \tag{3.2}$$

That is, the probability associated with the entire sample space is unity. The second condition on P is

$$E_1 \cap E_2 = \phi \Rightarrow P(E_1 \cup E_2) = P(E_1) + P(E_2). \tag{3.3}$$

That is, the probability associated with the union of two disjoint events, E_1 and E_2, is the arithmetical sum of the probabilities of E_1 and E_2 individually. From these primitive concepts, definitions and axioms it is then possible to derive the entire body of theorems concerning probability.

In this form probability calculus is simply an abstract formal deductive system. In order that this abstract system may be applied to problems of decision-making it requires an *interpretation* that will consist essentially of a procedure for specifying (a) what empirical entities are to count as simple events; (b) which subsets of the sample space constitute the relevant events for a particular experiment and (c) how probabilities are to be associated with empirical events.

For the objective probability (or relative frequency) school the appropriate procedure for associating probabilities with events consists of identifying probabilities with the limit of relative frequencies in repeated trials of an experiment, the outcomes of which are the real interpretation of the abstract 'events' of mathematical probability. Of course it is only possible to observe the outcomes of a *finite* number of repeated trials of a particular experiment, so that the relative frequency school *estimates* the limit of relative frequency from sample data. It follows that if *either* a decision-making situation cannot be regarded as an instance of repeated trials of a given experiment (e.g. a bet on the outcome of a general election) *or* if a decision-making situation *can* be so regarded but no sample data exist, then such a situation cannot be analysed with the tools of objective probability. The range of decision-making situations in which degrees of belief can be described in terms of objective probabilities is therefore rather limited.

In contrast, the advocates of the *subjective* view of probability require no such link between probability and observed relative frequency. At its most general level the subjective view of probability simply postulates that the ordering over states of the world in terms of degrees of belief is representable by a real-valued function which behaves like the function P of mathematical probability theory. Thus, for example, the subjective probability associated with the occurrence of one or other of a pair of mutually exclusive states of the world, s_1 and s_2, will be the arithmetical sum of the subjective probabilities associated with s_1 and s_2 individually. Apart from the requirement that subjective probabilities 'behave like' the probability measure of the abstract mathematical system, advocates of the subjective probability approach place no further *a priori* restrictions on the relationship between empirical evidence (such as historical frequencies) and subjective probabilities. (It should be noted, however, that for subjective probabilists who are also Bayesians there are prescribed procedures for *adjusting* subjective probabilities in the light of *new* empirical evidence.[5]) It is clear, then, that there is *no a priori* restriction upon the range of decision-making situations in which degrees of belief may be formalised as subjective probabilities.[6]

Shackle's formalisation of degrees of belief in terms of 'degrees of potential surprise'[7] (rather than subjective or objective probabilities) arises from his introspective evaluation of how the human mind actually views problems of uncertainty. Shackle argues that the procedure by which individuals assess their degrees of belief in any particular consequence of an action is by imagining how surprised they would feel if that specific consequence were to occur. Consequences with high degrees of potential surprise are clearly judged 'unlikely' to occur while those with low degrees of potential surprise are judged 'likely'. The essential distinction between degrees of potential surprise and probabilities (subjective or objective) lies in the rules postulated for deriving the potential surprise associated with the occurrence of complex events. Thus, for example, the potential surprise of a pair of mutually exclusive events E_1 and E_2 is the *lower* of the degrees of potential surprise associated with E_1 and E_2 individually. Degrees of potential surprise therefore behave quite unlike probabilities, and it is something of a paradox that, while Shackle rejects probabilistic descriptions of degrees of belief on introspective and intuitive grounds, his suggested alternative has failed to find popularity precisely because of its strangeness and lack of correspondence with the more familiar probability concepts.[8]

The last of the four major procedures for describing degrees of belief in the occurrence of different states of the world is *not* to give any formal description, but simply to 'represent' the preference ordering over actions by a utility function defined on the set of n-tuples of contingent consequences and then let implicit degrees of belief be reflected in the form of this utility function. Thus suppose, for example, that there are just two states of the world, s_1 and s_2, and that contingent consequences are levels of profit so that they may be described by real numbers. The utility function would then reflect a (say) high degree of belief in the occurrence of s_1 by requiring a relatively large increase in c_{i2} to compensate for a unit fall in c_{i1}.

The problem with this procedure is that, while degrees of belief are given no *explicit* formalisation in the description of a decision-making situation, it is nonetheless necessary to take *implicit* account of the decision-maker's confidence in the occurrence of the various states of the world in order to specify the properties of the utility function over contingent consequences. It seems inevitable that, if one does not have a formal description of degrees of belief, there is a danger that specification of the utility function will become a more or less arbitrary exercise.

Suppose that one or other of the above procedures has been adopted as a means of providing a formal description of degrees of belief in the occurrence of the various states of the world. Development of a theory of choice under uncertainty then requires specification of the way in which contingent consequences and degrees of belief determine the preference ordering over alternative actions. Without doubt the most common approach to the analysis of choice under uncertainty is to formalise degrees of belief as subjective probabilities and then to employ the so-called 'expected-utility' theory of choice to relate the preference ordering over actions to contingent consequences and degrees of belief. In essence, the expected utility theorem asserts the existence of a real-valued utility function (unique up to a positive linear transformation) on the set of consequences such that the preference ordering over actions is representable by the *mathematical expectation* of utility for each action.[9] Since the bulk of the analysis in the remainder of this book is based upon the subjective probability/expected utility approach, the next section is devoted to development and discussion of the Expected Utility Theorem.

II THE EXPECTED UTILITY THEOREM[10]

Consider two actions, $a_1 = (c_{11}, c_{12}, \ldots c_{1n})$ and $a_2 = (c_{21}, c_{22}, \ldots c_{2n})$, such that

$$
\left.
\begin{aligned}
c_{1j} &= c_{2j} \ (j = 1 \ldots n, j \neq k, h) \\
c_{1k} &= c_{2h} \\
c_{1h} &= c_{2k}
\end{aligned}
\right\} \tag{3.4}
$$

(where the assertion that two contingent consequences are equal is to be interpreted as meaning that they are identical in every respect, except for the state of the world under which they occur). Throughout the discussion that follows it will be assumed that if the subjective probability associated with s_k is equal to the subjective probability associated with s_h then the decision-maker is *indifferent* between a_1 and a_2. This assumption is equivalent to indifference concerning the states of the world *per se* — that is, the decision-maker does not care under which state of the world a given consequence[11] occurs.

Given this assumption, each action is completely specified by a subjective probability distribution of consequences without any necessity for information concerning the states of the world under which such consequences occur. For example, consider the following array of contingent consequences where the subjective probabilities associated with states are shown in parentheses. For simplicity there are taken to be just two types of consequence, $\tilde{c}$ and $\bar{c}$.

	$s_1(0.6)$	$s_2(0.3)$	$s_3(0.1)$
a_1	$\bar{c}$	$\tilde{c}$	$\bar{c}$
a_2	$\tilde{c}$	$\bar{c}$	$\tilde{c}$
a_3	$\bar{c}$	$\bar{c}$	$\tilde{c}$

Given the assumption of indifference between states of the world *per se*, *all* relevant information concerning this decision-making situation is contained in the subjective probability distribution corresponding to each action:

$$a_1 \quad : \quad \begin{bmatrix} \bar{c} & \tilde{c} \\ 0.7 & 0.3 \end{bmatrix}$$

$$a_2 \quad : \quad \begin{bmatrix} \bar{c} & \tilde{c} \\ 0.3 & 0.7 \end{bmatrix}$$

$$a_3 \quad : \quad \begin{bmatrix} \bar{c} & \tilde{c} \\ 0.9 & 0.1 \end{bmatrix}$$

(Throughout this section all probability distributions will be written as $2 \times n$ arrays or, where consequences are reals, as $2 \times n$ matrices.)

Hence, the preference ordering over actions may be thought of as a preference ordering over *subjective probability distributions of consequences*. We therefore proceed to define a relation, R, ('being preferred or indifferent to') on the set, $\mathscr{D}$, of subjective probability distributions of consequences. R will be assumed to satisfy the following axioms.

Axiom 1. R is reflexive, non-symmetric, transitive and connected.[1][2]

The relations 'being indifferent to', I, and 'being preferred to', P, are then defined in terms of R as follows.
For all $d_1, d_2 \in \mathscr{D}$,

(a) $\qquad\qquad d_1 I d_2 \equiv d_1 R d_2 \quad and \quad d_2 R d_1$ $\qquad\qquad$ (3.5)

(b) $\qquad\qquad d_1 P d_2 \equiv d_1 R d_2 \quad and\ not \quad d_2 R d_1.$ $\qquad\qquad$ (3.6)

It follows immediately that I is reflexive, symmetric and transitive while P is irreflexive, asymmetric and transitive. In addition, it is fairly easy to prove that the following lemma is implied by Axiom 1 and the definitions of P and I.

Ordering lemma. For all $d_1, d_2, d_3, d_4 \in \mathscr{D}$,

$$d_1 P d_2 \quad and \quad d_1 I d_3 \quad and \quad d_2 I d_4 \Rightarrow d_3 P d_4.$$ $\qquad$ (3.7)

Notice that since particular consequences 'with certainty' are simply degenerate probability distributions, the relations R, P and I are well defined on the set of consequences with certainty. From a notational point of view, c_k $(k = 1 \ldots r)$ will normally denote consequences. However when the c_k are written with R, P or I they are to be interpreted as denoting consequences *with certainty*. Thus for example $c_1 P c_2$ is to be interpreted as meaning that the action giving rise to c_1 with certainty is preferred to the action giving rise to c_2 with certainty.

Axiom 2.   For all c_1, c_2 and c_3, there exists an unique p such that

$$c_1 R c_2 \text{ and } c_2 R c_3 \text{ and } c_1 P c_3 \Rightarrow c_2 I \begin{bmatrix} c_1 & c_3 \\ p & (1-p) \end{bmatrix}. \tag{3.8}$$

Axiom 3.   For all c_1 and c_2,

$$c_1 P c_2 \Rightarrow \left(p > q \Leftrightarrow \begin{bmatrix} c_1 & c_2 \\ p & (1-p) \end{bmatrix} P \begin{bmatrix} c_1 & c_2 \\ q & (1-q) \end{bmatrix} \right). \tag{3.9}$$

Axiom 4

$$\left. c_k I \begin{bmatrix} \tilde{c} & \bar{c} \\ \pi_k & (1-\pi_k) \end{bmatrix}, (k = 1 \ldots r) \Rightarrow \begin{bmatrix} c_1 & c_2 \ldots c_r \\ p_1 & p_2 \ldots p_r \end{bmatrix} I \begin{bmatrix} \tilde{c} & \bar{c} \\ q & (1-q) \end{bmatrix} \right\}$$

where

$$q = \sum_k p_k \pi_k.$$

$$\tag{3.10}$$

Axioms 1—3 have such strong and immediate intuitive appeal that they would seem to warrant no detailed explanation. The rationale for axiom 4 is, however, not so obvious. In essence, this axiom embodies the idea that if $c_k I d_k$ $(k = 1 \ldots r)$ then the decision-maker will be indifferent between a subjective distribution

$$\begin{bmatrix} c_1 & c_2 \ldots c_r \\ p_1 & p_2 \ldots p_r \end{bmatrix}$$

and another subjective distribution

$$\begin{bmatrix} d_1 & d_2 \ldots d_r \\ p_1 & p_2 \ldots p_r \end{bmatrix}$$

in which $d_1 \ldots d_r$ are to be regarded as *conditional* subjective distributions. If this is the case *and* if marginal subjective probabilities are conventionally related to conditional subjective probabilities, then (3.10) will hold.

From axioms 1—4 it is possible to prove the following theorem.

Expected Utility Theorem. There exists a real-valued utility function, U, on the set of consequences such that for all

$$d_1 = \begin{bmatrix} c_1 & c_2 & \ldots c_k & \ldots \\ p_{11} & p_{12} & \ldots p_{1k} & \ldots \end{bmatrix}$$

and

$$d_2 = \begin{bmatrix} c_1 & c_2 & \ldots c_k & \ldots \\ p_{21} & p_{22} & \ldots p_{2k} & \ldots \end{bmatrix}$$

$$\sum_k p_{1k} U(c_k) > \sum_k p_{2k} U(c_k) \Leftrightarrow d_1 P d_2. \tag{3.11}$$

In addition, any positive linear transformation of U also satisfies (3.11).

The first step in the proof of this theorem is to show that it is *always* possible to find subjective probability distributions

$$\begin{bmatrix} \tilde{c} & \bar{c} \\ \pi_k & (1 - \pi_k) \end{bmatrix}$$

satisfying the antecedent condition in (3.10). To do this, define $\tilde{c}$ and $\bar{c}$ such that, *for all k,*

and
$$\left. \begin{array}{c} \tilde{c} R c_k \\[2mm] c_k R \bar{c}. \end{array} \right\} \tag{3.12}$$

In addition, provided the decision-making situation is non-trivial, we shall have,

$$\tilde{c} P \bar{c}. \tag{3.13}$$

$\tilde{c}$ and $\bar{c}$ may therefore be thought of as the 'best' and 'worst' possible consequences respectively.

From axiom 2 it then follows that for each c_k there exists an unique π_k such that

$$c_k I \begin{bmatrix} \tilde{c} & \bar{c} \\ \pi_k & (1 - \pi_k) \end{bmatrix}. \tag{3.14}$$

Now consider the subjective probability distributions d_1 and d_2 of the theorem. From axiom 4 and (3.14) we have

$$d_1 I \begin{bmatrix} \tilde{c} & \bar{c} \\ q_1 & (1 - q_1) \end{bmatrix} \tag{3.15}$$

where

$$q_1 = \sum_k p_{1k} \pi_k \tag{3.16}$$

and

$$d_2 I \begin{bmatrix} \tilde{c} & \bar{c} \\ q_2 & (1 - q_2) \end{bmatrix} \tag{3.17}$$

where

$$q_2 = \sum_k p_{2k} \pi_k . \tag{3.18}$$

But by axiom 3 together with the definition of $\tilde{c}$ and $\bar{c}$,

$$\begin{bmatrix} \tilde{c} & \bar{c} \\ q_1 & (1 - q_1) \end{bmatrix} P \begin{bmatrix} \tilde{c} & \bar{c} \\ q_2 & (1 - q_2) \end{bmatrix} \Leftrightarrow q_1 > q_2 . \tag{3.19}$$

Thus by (3.15)–(3.19) together with the Ordering Lemma,

$$\sum_k p_{1k} \pi_k > \sum_k p_{2k} \pi_k \Leftrightarrow d_1 P d_2 . \tag{3.20}$$

Thus, if for all k we let

$$U(c_k) = \pi_k \tag{3.21}$$

the first part of the Expected Utility Theorem is proved. Now define a function U^t by

$$U^t(c_k) = \alpha + \beta U(c_k), \quad \beta > 0. \tag{3.22}$$

Hence,

$$\sum_k p_{1k} U^t(c_k) > \sum_k p_{2k} U^t(c_k) \Leftrightarrow \sum_k p_{1k} U(c_k) > \sum_k p_{2k} U(c_k). \tag{3.23}$$

The second part of the theorem follows from (3.20) and (3.23).

Throughout this section it has been implicitly assumed that the set of consequences is either finite or countably infinite. It is clear, though, that for those cases in which consequences are levels of wealth, income or profit (for example) it will be more natural to represent the set of consequences by some interval on the real line. In such cases the set of consequences will be non-countably infinite and the above analysis is not applicable. However, with slight modification axiom 4 can be made relevant to continuous as well as discrete distributions, thereby removing the limitation on the analysis.

So far the discussion in this section has been exclusively concerned with the *preference* ordering, nothing having been said about *choice* as such. *In order to make an explicit connection between preference and choice it will be assumed that the action that is chosen is preferred or indifferent to every other feasible action.* It then follows that any decision-maker whose preference ordering over actions obeys axioms 1—4 will *always* choose that action which maximises expected utility (for any utility function that is a positive linear transformation of the function given in (3.21)). That is, the decision-maker will behave as though he were an 'expected utility maximiser'.

III   CONDITIONAL UTILITY FUNCTIONS

In the preceding discussion the concept of a consequence has been quite deliberately made as general as possible. Thus, the Expected Utility Theorem is relevant not only to situations in which consequences can be simply described by real numbers, but also to situations in which the complete specification of consequences involves characteristics of the decision-maker's environment *incapable* of adequate description in terms of the reals.

In the next two chapters we shall be concerned particularly with decision-making situations in which the specification of consequences requires information concerning:

(a) the level of wealth with which an individual commences a particular period of time; *and*
(b) whether or not the individual lives through that period of time.

Any such consequence can be completely specified by an ordered pair, the first component of which is a real number describing the level of wealth and the second component a statement indicating whether the individual survives or dies during the relevant period; i.e.

$$c_k = (w_k, h_k) \tag{3.24}$$

where $w_k \in \mathbf{R}$, $h_k \in \{\varsigma, \theta\}$, ς denoting 'life' and θ denoting 'death'.

In this situation, then, the utility function U is a real-valued function on the set of these ordered pairs. Let us now define two real-valued functions $L(w_k)$ and $D(w_k)$ as follows:

$$L(w_k) \equiv U(w_k, \varsigma) \tag{3.25}$$

$$D(w_k) \equiv U(w_k, \theta). \tag{3.26}$$

$L(w_k)$ may therefore be thought of as a utility of wealth function *conditional on survival of the relevant time period*, while $D(w_k)$ may be thought of as a utility of wealth function *conditional on death during the relevant period*.

Now consider a situation in which an individual has no uncertainty about the level of wealth, w, with which he is to commence a given period of time but *is* uncertain about whether or not he will survive the period, attaching a subjective probability, p, to the outcome of his death during the period. The expected utility for this situation may then be written as

$$E(U) = (1 - p)U(w, \varsigma) + pU(w, \theta) \tag{3.27}$$

$$= (1 - p)L(w) \quad + pD(w). \tag{3.28}$$

An alternative approach to the development of conditional utility functions is to regard specification of such matters as survival or death as essential features of a description of the states of the world discussed in section I above. Under these circumstances it becomes necessary to drop the assumption of indifference between states (see section II) and to assume instead that the individual has a preference ordering over states *per se*. This is essentially the approach pioneered by Hirshleifer (1965, 1966). The major disadvantage of this approach is that, if it is to be used to analyse situations in which the probability of outcomes such as survival are under the control of the decision-maker, then it is also necessary to drop the assumption of parametric subjective probabilities for alternative states of the world.[13]

IV   THE SOURCE OF SUBJECTIVE PROBABILITIES

In section I of this chapter subjective probabilities were introduced as a means of formalising an individual's degrees of belief in the occurrence of various states of the world. However, no justification was given for this formalisation, other than its generality and intuitive appeal relative to alternative formalisations of degrees of belief.

Fortunately it is possible to give the concept of subjective probability a rather more rigorous foundation, as a number of writers — notably Ramsey (1931), Savage (1954) and De Finetti (1958) — have demonstrated. In essence these writers have shown that, provided the preference ordering over alternative actions obeys a limited number of very plausible axioms, then it is possible to associate real numbers $p(s_j)$ with states and $U(c_k)$ with consequences such that the $p(s_j)$ satisfy the axioms of mathematical probability and the $U(c_k)$ — in conjunction with the $p(s_j)$ — satisfy the Expected Utility Theorem. Furthermore it seems natural to define a relation 'being judged more probable than' in the following way: consider two actions $a_1 = (c_{11}, c_{12}, \ldots c_{1n})$ and $a_2 = (c_{21}, c_{22}, \ldots c_{2n})$ such that[14]

$$\left. \begin{array}{l} c_{1j} = c_{2j}, \ (j = 1 \ldots n, j \neq k, h) \\ c_{1k} = c_{2h} = c_a \\ c_{1h} = c_{2k} = c_b \\ c_a \ P \ c_b . \end{array} \right\} \tag{3.29}$$

Then s_k is said to be 'judged more probable than' s_h if and only if $a_1 \ P \ a_2$. It can be shown that the ordering of states of the world by this relation is *precisely the same* as the ordering by the $p(s_j)$. This confirms the interpretation of the $p(s_j)$ as subjective probabilities.

Needless to say, the formal proof of these propositions is not particularly easy and it is for this reason that it was felt preferable simply to *assume* the existence of subjective probabilities in this chapter.

NOTATIONAL GLOSSARY

a_i the ith action
s_j the jth state of the world
c_{ij} the contingent consequence for the ith action and jth state
c_k the kth consequence
$\tilde{c}, \bar{c}$ consequences
E_1, E_2 events
p, q, π subjective probabilities
d_i the subjective probability distribution of consequences for the ith action
w_k the wealth associated with the kth consequence

h_k the environment for the kth consequence ($h_k = \zeta$ denotes 'life' and $h_k = \theta$ denotes 'death')

S the sample space

$\mathbf{R}$ the set of real numbers

$\mathscr{C}$ the class of subsets of the sample space

$\mathscr{D}$ the set of subjective probability distributions

R the relation of 'being preferred or indifferent to'

P the relation of 'being preferred to'

I the relation of 'being indifferent to'

P the probability function from $\mathscr{C}$ to $[0, 1]$

U a real valued utility function defined on the set of consequences

U^t a positive linear transformation of U

NOTES

1. Two excellent general works dealing with some of the topics considered in this chapter are Arrow (1971) and Kyburg and Smokler (1964).
2. Since some allocative adjustments may involve *increases* in risk for some individuals, it will also be important to consider the minimum sums that such individuals would require in *compensation*.
3. The traditional distinction between risk and uncertainty (due originally to Knight (1921)) reserves the term 'risk' for those situations in which the language of probability theory may legitimately be employed and the term 'uncertainty' for situations in which it may not. For advocates of the *subjective* probability approach outlined below the distinction is not very fruitful since *all* situations in which the consequences of actions are not known with certainty may be analysed in terms of probability concepts (albeit *subjective*) provided only that the decision-maker's choices conform to the appropriate axioms. (The risk—uncertainty distinction might be maintained by reserving the term 'risk' for those choices in which probabilities are taken to be 'objective' — i.e. identified with relative frequencies — but this does not seem to be a particularly fruitful or popular semantic convention). Consequently, the terms 'risk' and 'uncertainty' are used synonymously in the remainder of this book.
4. Alternatively, actions may be considered as *functions* from the set of states into the set of consequences.
5. See, for example, Ozga (1965) pp. 72—5.
6. i.e. there is no particular *type* of decision-making situation in which a subjective probability formalisation of degrees of belief is inappropriate for *everyone*. It may of course be that for certain individuals such formalisation is inappropriate in view of the peculiarities of their degrees of belief (e.g. someone for whom the relation 'being judged more probable' is intransitive).
7. Shackle (1949). For an illuminating critical evaluation of Shackle's ideas, see Ozga (1965) chapter 7.

8. In addition, the rules for deriving the potential surprise associated with complex events have rather strange implications. Consider an experiment involving two tosses of a 'fair' coin. The potential surprise associated with the sequence 'heads, heads' would, for most people, (a) *exceed* the potential surprise for the non-occurrence of this sequence and (b) *equal* the potential surprise for any other particular sequence. One would therefore expect the rule for deriving the potential surprise of the non-occurrence of the sequence 'heads, heads' to reflect this property. However, the potential surprise of the non-occurrence of the sequence 'heads, heads' is the *lowest* potential surprise of any of the various sequences other than 'heads, heads'. Hence under Shackle's rules the potential surprise of the non-occurrence of 'heads, heads' *equals* the potential surprise of the occurrence of the sequence.

9. i.e. action a_1 will be preferred to action a_2 *if and only if* the mathematical expectation of utility for a_1 exceeds the mathematical expectation of utility for a_2.

10. The proof of the Expected Utility Theorem presented in this section is basically similar to that given by Luce and Raiffa (1967). The essential difference between the two proofs is that the one presented here (being explicitly developed in terms of the concept of consequences contingent on states of the world) defines a preference ordering on subjective distributions of *consequences*, whereas Luce and Raiffa's preference ordering is over '*lottery tickets*', the latter being probability distributions of outcomes where an outcome may *itself* be a probability distribution. It seemed unnatural to allow the set of consequences to include probability distributions in view of the earlier definition of a state of the world as a description of the world assigning a *determinate* consequence to each alternative action. It is essentially for this reason that axiom 4 is presented in a relatively obscure form. For examples of other proofs that (like the one presented here) do *not* axiomatise subjective probability see Von Neumann and Morgenstern (1953), Markowitz (1959), Baumol (1965) and Arrow (1971). Of these, the proof by Von Neumann and Morgenstern is the most widely quoted and (like those given by Markowitz and Arrow) is rather more rigorous and elegant than that presented in this chapter. By contrast Baumol's proof is rather informal but represents an excellent introduction to the subject.

11. A consequence — in contrast to a *contingent* consequence — carries no specification of the state of the world in which it occurs.

12. That is,
    (a) for all i, $d_i R d_i$ (reflexivity);
    (b) for some $d_i \neq d_f$, $d_i R d_f$ and $d_f R d_i$, while for some $d_e \neq d_g$, $d_e R d_g$ and not $d_g R d_e$ (non-symmetry);
    (c) for all d_i, d_f, d_g, $d_i R d_f$ and $d_f R d_g \Rightarrow d_i R d_g$ (transitivity);
    (d) for all d_i, d_f, $d_i R d_f$ or $d_f R d_i$ (connectedness).

13. For a rigorous development of this type of approach to the problem of choice under uncertainty, see Luce and Krantz (1971).

14. The meaning of the 'equality' of two contingent consequences is as earlier defined, while $c_a P c_b$ is to be interpreted as meaning that an action giving c_a in every state of the world is preferred to an action giving c_b in every state of the world (i.e. the certainty of c_a is preferred to the certainty of c_b).

REFERENCES

Arrow, K. J. *Essays in the Theory of Risk Bearing* London, North Holland (1971)

De Finetti, B. 'Foundations of Probability' *Philosophy in the Mid-Century* Florence, La Nuova Italia Editrice (1958)

Baumol, W. J. *Economic Theory and Operations Analysis* Englewood Cliffs New Jersey, Prentice Hall (1965)

Hirshleifer, J. 'Investment Decisions Under Uncertainty—Choice—Theoretic Approaches' *Quarterly Journal of Economics* (November 1965)

Hirshleifer, J. 'Investment Decision Under Uncertainty: Applications of the State Preference Approach' *Quarterly Journal of Economics* (May 1966)

Kyburg, H. E. and Smokler, H. E. *Studies in Subjective Probability* New York, Wiley (1964)

Knight, F. R. *Risk Uncertainty and Profit* Boston and New York, Houghton Mifflin (1921)

Luce, R. D. and Krantz, D. H. 'Conditional Expected Utility' *Econometrica* (March 1971)

Luce, R. D. and Raiffa, H. 'An Axiomatic Treatment of Utility' in W. Edwards and A. Tversky (eds.) *Decision Making* Harmondsworth, Penguin (1967)

Markowitz, H. M. *Portfolio Selection* New York, Wiley (1959)

Ozga, S. A. *Expectations in Economic Theory* London, Weidenfeld and Nicolson (1965)

Ramsey, F. P. *The Foundations of Mathematics and Other Logical Essays* London, Kegan Paul (1931)

Savage, L. J. *The Foundations of Statistics* New York, Wiley (1954)

Shackle, G. L. S. *Expectation in Economics* Cambridge, University Press (1949)

Von Neumann, J. and Morgenstern, O. *Theory of Games and Economic Behavior* Princeton, University Press (1953)

4. Optimal Expenditure on Life Insurance

In essence, a life insurance (or life 'assurance'[1]) contract consists of a legal arrangement between an insurance company and an individual (the 'owner') in which the latter undertakes to make one or more premium payments in return for which the insurance company agrees to pay a given sum (the 'sum assured') to the estate of the owner, or to a beneficiary nominated by him, in the event of the death of a particular person (the 'insured') during a period of time specified in the insurance contract. The contract period may be the entire lifetime of the insured ('whole-life' insurance) or a period of n years ('n-year term' insurance). In addition it is possible to enter into 'endowment' insurance contracts whereby the beneficiary receives the sum assured at the *earlier* date of either the death of the insured or the term specified in the insurance contract. Throughout the present chapter we shall be exclusively concerned with those cases in which the owner and insured are one and the same person.

It is clear, then, that the existence of an opportunity to enter into a life insurance contract allows an individual to purchase a *contingent* increment in the wealth of his heirs, his own death being the contingency upon which the increment depends. Consequently it is not surprising that such contracts are primarily held by individuals whose wages or salaries are the major source of family income and whose premature demise would, therefore, inevitably involve a considerable reduction in the standard of living of surviving dependants. Life insurance provides any such individual with the opportunity to purchase a reduction in the *distastefulness* of the prospect of his own premature death to the extent that it permits him to avoid (or at least to mitigate) the reduction in his dependants' income that would otherwise occur should be die. Thus, by permitting an individual to alter the *consequences* associated with the event of his death, it appears that life insurance will play an important if indirect part in determining the value placed by the individual on changes in the risk of death. For this reason the present chapter is devoted to a discussion of the individual decision concerning optimal expenditure of life insurance.

Initially, the analysis is developed within a highly simplified, single-period framework: this facilitates the introduction of a number of important concepts. The analysis is then generalised to continuous time in section IV.

I   TERM INSURANCE: THE BASIC MODEL

Let us begin by considering a very simple discrete-time situation in which an individual associates a subjective probability $\bar{p}$ with the outcome of his death during the current period. It will be assumed that $0 < \bar{p} < 1$ and (as is usual in discrete-time analyses) that the individual does not distinguish between the various instants of time within the current period.

The individual's decision-making under uncertainty will be taken to conform to the axioms of the previous chapter so that he will behave as if he were an expected utility-maximiser. Furthermore, if the individual has no uncertainty concerning the level of wealth,[2] $\bar{w}$, with which he is to commence the current period then, following the analysis of section III of chapter 3, his expected utility may be written as

$$E(U) = (1 - \bar{p})L(\bar{w}) + \bar{p}D(\bar{w}). \tag{4.1}$$

It must be stressed that the fact that the arguments of both $L(w)$ and $D(w)$ are written as $\bar{w}$ in (4.1) is *not* intended to imply that the individual's heirs will inherit *all* of $\bar{w}$ (death duties and the elimination of human wealth will both tend to reduce the amount of wealth capable of being bequeathed below $\bar{w}$). It is important to remember that $D(w)$ was defined as a function giving the utility of *initial* wealth conditional on death during the relevant period (i.e., $D(w)$ gives the utility index corresponding to that situation in which the individual *starts* the period with wealth w and expects to die *during* the period). It would of course be possible to define a function giving the utility index of bequeathable (rather than initial) wealth conditional on death. For example, suppose that bequeathable wealth, ω, is related to initial wealth w by

$$\omega = b(w). \tag{4.2}$$

A utility function for bequeathable wealth, $F(\omega)$, may then be defined as

$$F(\omega) \equiv D[b^{-1}(\omega)] \tag{4.3}$$

where $b^{-1}(\omega)$ is the inverse of $b(w)$.

Since there seems to be no great advantage in working with $F(\omega)$ thus defined, the analysis will be developed on the basis of the more straightforward concept of the function $D(w)$.

Now suppose that the individual is offered the opportunity to purchase *term insurance* for the current period by making a premium payment at the beginning of the period. We shall denote the premium by x, the gross sum assured by y and the *net* sum assured $(y - x)$ by z. For simplicity it will be assumed that x is proportional to y so that

$$z = kx \ (k > 0) \tag{4.4}$$

If the individual spends a sum, x, on insurance then, provided that he survives the current period, his initial wealth is simply $\bar{w} - x$. If, however, the individual dies during the current period then his estate is augmented by the net sum assured, z, at the time of his death and, since we are not distinguishing the instants of time during the current period, his initial wealth is given by $\bar{w} + z$. Thus if the individual purchases life insurance then the level of his initial wealth is *itself* contingent upon whether or not the individual survives the current period. The individual's optimal (and hence, by assumption, *chosen*) expenditure on insurance[3] will therefore be given by the solution of

$$\text{Max}_{x} \ E(U) = (1 - \bar{p})L(\bar{w} - x) + \bar{p}D(\bar{w} + z)$$

subject to

$$\tag{4.5}$$

$$0 \leqslant x \leqslant \bar{w}.$$

Assuming that $L(w)$ and $D(w)$ are both differentiable functions; then, at the optimum, *either*

$$\frac{\partial E(U)}{\partial x} \leqslant 0 \quad \text{and} \quad x \frac{\partial E(U)}{\partial x} = 0 \tag{4.6}$$

or

$$\frac{\partial E(U)}{\partial x} \geqslant 0 \quad \text{and} \quad (\bar{w} - x) \frac{\partial E(U)}{\partial x} = 0. \tag{4.7}$$

Thus from (4.4), (4.5), (4.6) and (4.7) the optimal value of x must satisfy the following conditions:

either

$$(1 - \bar{p}) \frac{\partial L(\bar{w} - x)}{\partial x} + k\bar{p} \frac{\partial D(\bar{w} + z)}{\partial z} \leqslant 0$$

and

$$x \left[(1 - \bar{p}) \frac{\partial L(\bar{w} - x)}{\partial x} + k\bar{p} \frac{\partial D(\bar{w} + z)}{\partial z} \right] = 0$$

$$(4.8)$$

or

$$(1 - \bar{p}) \frac{\partial L(\bar{w} - x)}{\partial x} + k\bar{p} \frac{\partial D(\bar{w} + z)}{\partial z} \geqslant 0$$

and

$$(\bar{w} - x) \left[(1 - \bar{p}) \frac{\partial L(\bar{w} - x)}{\partial x} + k\bar{p} \frac{\partial D(\bar{w} + z)}{\partial z} \right] = 0.$$

$$(4.9)$$

(4.8) and (4.9) give the necessary conditions for maximising expected utility with respect to insurance expenditure and are expressed in terms of $L(w)$ and $D(w)$ evaluated at $w = \bar{w} - x$ and $w = \bar{w} + z$ respectively. However, it is also possible to establish necessary and sufficient conditions for the purchase of a *positive* amount of insurance in terms of $L(w)$ and $D(w)$ *both evaluated at* $w = \bar{w}$. Since the latter conditions will play an important part in subsequent analysis it is important to consider them in some detail. However, it will greatly simplify the derivation and statement of these conditions if we can place further plausible restrictions on the properties of $L(w)$ and $D(w)$, and the next section is therefore devoted to the development of such restrictions.

II   FURTHER RESTRICTIONS ON THE PROPERTIES OF $L(w)$ AND $D(w)$

So far the only assumption that has been made concerning $L(w)$ and $D(w)$ is that both functions are differentiable. The argument that follows will be based upon the slightly stronger assumption that both functions are at least *twice*-differentiable. In addition the majority of individuals will be taken to satisfy the following apparently reasonable assumptions.

(a) If the individual expects to survive the current period then he will be assumed to prefer to start the period with more wealth rather than less and also to be financially risk-averse.[4] $L(w)$ must therefore be *strictly* increasing and *strictly* concave; that is

$$\frac{dL}{dw} > 0 \tag{4.10}$$

and

$$\frac{d^2 L}{dw^2} < 0. \tag{4.11}$$

(b) The individual will be assumed *not* to be misanthropic to his heirs and also *not* to wish them more rather than less financial risk, so that $D(w)$ must be non-decreasing and concave; that is

$$\frac{dD}{dw} \geqslant 0 \tag{4.12}$$

and

$$\frac{d^2 D}{dw^2} \leqslant 0. \tag{4.13}$$

(c) It will be assumed that for each level of initial wealth the individual prefers to live rather than die during the current period so that for all w

$$L(w) > D(w). \tag{4.14}$$

(d) In order to avoid versions of the St Petersburg Paradox[5] it is necessary to assumes that $L(w)$ is bounded *above* and that $D(w)$ is bounded *below*. (4.14) then ensures that $L(w)$ is also bounded below and $D(w)$ bounded above.[6]

It should be noted that, while upper-boundedness of $L(w)$ and $D(w)$ is perfectly consistent with the other assumptions adopted in this section, lower-boundedness of $L(w)$ and $D(w)$ appears to require modification to (4.11) and (4.13) for small values of w unless the *domains* of $L(w)$ and $D(w)$ are themselves bounded below by, for example, zero, in which case the lower bound of $L(w)$ is (trivially) $L(0)$. For this reason whenever there exists no lower bound for w then the analysis is to be taken as being relevant only for values of w for which (4.11) and (4.13) *do*, in fact, hold. This will usually not represent a severe restriction.

III NECESSARY AND SUFFICIENT CONDITIONS FOR THE PURCHASE OF TERM INSURANCE

Let us now develop the necessary and sufficient conditions for the purchase of term insurance within the context of the single-period model introduced in section I above. We shall do this by explicitly considering the relationship between $E(U)$ and x.

From (4.5),

$$\frac{\partial E(U)}{\partial x} = (1 - \bar{p}) \frac{\partial L(\bar{w} - x)}{\partial x} + k\bar{p} \frac{\partial D(\bar{w} + z)}{\partial z} \qquad (4.15)$$

and in particular

$$\frac{\partial E(U)}{\partial x}\bigg|_{x=0} = -(1 - \bar{p}) \frac{dL}{dw}\bigg|_{w=\bar{w}} + k\bar{p} \frac{dD}{dw}\bigg|_{w=\bar{w}}. \qquad (4.16)$$

But from (4.10) and (4.11),

$$x > 0 \Rightarrow \frac{\partial L(\bar{w} - x)}{\partial x} < -\frac{dL}{dw}\bigg|_{w=\bar{w}} \qquad (4.17)$$

and from (4.12) and (4.13)

$$z > 0 \Rightarrow \frac{\partial D(\bar{w} + z)}{\partial z} < \frac{dD}{dw}\bigg|_{w=\bar{w}}. \qquad (4.18)$$

Hence, from (4.15), (4.16), (4.17) and (4.18)

$$\frac{\partial E(U)}{\partial x}\bigg|_{x=0} \leqslant 0 \Rightarrow \frac{\partial E(U)}{\partial x}\bigg|_{x>0} < 0, \qquad (4.19)$$

$$\frac{\partial E(U)}{\partial x}\bigg|_{x=0} > 0 \Rightarrow \frac{\partial E(U)}{\partial x}\bigg|_{x>0} \geqslant 0. \qquad (4.20)$$

Furthermore

$$\frac{\partial^2 E(U)}{\partial x^2} = (1 - \bar{p}) \frac{\partial^2 L(\bar{w} - x)}{\partial x^2} + k^2 \bar{p} \frac{\partial^2 D(\bar{w} + z)}{\partial z^2} \qquad (4.21)$$

so that, from (4.11), (4.13) and (4.21),

$$\frac{\partial^2 E(U)}{\partial x^2} < 0. \qquad (4.22)$$

The graph of the function relating $E(U)$ and x will therefore take one of the general forms depicted in figure 4.1.

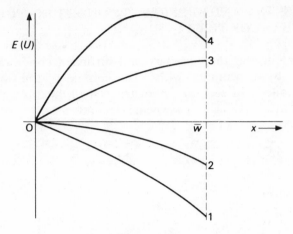

Figure 4.1.

Since the purchase of insurance raises $E(U)$ above the 'uninsured' level only in cases 3 and 4 in figure 4.1, it is clear that the *full necessary and sufficient* condition for the purchase of insurance is given by

$$\frac{\partial E(U)}{\partial x}\bigg|_{x=0} > 0 \tag{4.23}$$

or from (4.16)[7]

$$\frac{dL}{dw}\bigg|_{w=\bar{w}} < k\frac{\bar{p}}{1-\bar{p}}\frac{dD}{dw}\bigg|_{w=\bar{w}}. \tag{4.24}$$

Now insurance is normally categorised on the basis of the mathematical expectation of gain from purchasing the insurance. If this expectation is zero then the insurance is described as 'fair', if positive 'more than fair' and if negative 'less than fair'.[8] This categorisation therefore has an immediate counterpart in the relative magnitudes of k and $\bar{p}$:

Fair insurance: $\qquad\qquad k = \dfrac{1-\bar{p}}{\bar{p}}$

More than fair insurance: $\quad k > \dfrac{1-\bar{p}}{\bar{p}}$ $\qquad\qquad$ (4.25)

Less than fair insurance: $\quad k < \dfrac{1-\bar{p}}{\bar{p}}$

Given this taxonomy, a number of interesting points emerge concerning the purchase of insurance.

(a) If insurance is fair, then from (4.24) and (4.25) the necessary and sufficient condition for an individual to purchase insurance is given by

$$\frac{dL}{dw}\bigg|_{w=\bar{w}} < \frac{dD}{dw}\bigg|_{w=\bar{w}}. \tag{4.26}$$

That is, the individual will purchase fair insurance if and only if, prior to purchasing insurance, the marginal utility of wealth conditional on death exceeds the marginal utility of wealth conditional on survival. Clearly this condition will hold only if the individual 'cares' sufficiently that his heirs should be well provided for in the event of his death. Figure 4.2 depicts the form of the graphs of $L(w)$ and $D(w)$ in such a situation.

(b) If insurance is fair and the optimal expenditure on insurance x^* is such that

$$0 < x^* < \bar{w}, \tag{4.27}$$

then from (4.8), (4.9) and (4.25)

$$-\frac{\partial L(\bar{w} - x)}{\partial x} = \frac{\partial D(\bar{w} + z)}{\partial z}. \tag{4.28}$$

That is, if an individual purchases fair insurance in an amount less than his initial wealth, then he will do so up to the point at which the marginal utility of wealth conditional on survival equals the marginal utility of wealth conditional on death.

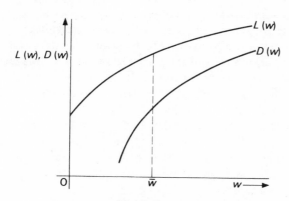

Figure 4.2.

(c) If insurance is either fair or less than fair then it will not be purchased by anyone for whom the following condition holds,

$$\left.\frac{dL}{dw}\right|_{w=\bar{w}} \geqslant \left.\frac{dD}{dw}\right|_{w=\bar{w}}. \tag{4.29}$$

That is, fair or less than fair insurance will not be purchased if, without insurance, the marginal utility of wealth conditional on survival exceeds or equals the marginal utility of wealth conditional on death.

(d) Suppose that $D(w)$ is constant. It then follows from (4.10) and (4.24) that, given $k > 0$ and $0 < \bar{p} < 1$, *no* insurance will be purchased. This result is hardly surprising when one remembers that if $D(w)$ is constant then the individual is literally *indifferent* to the amount of wealth that his heirs inherit and will therefore not be prepared to reduce his wealth contingent on survival for any increase (however large) in wealth contingent on death. The most obvious example of this situation is the bachelor with no dependent relatives who is also indifferent to the welfare of those who survive him.

IV   A CONTINUOUS-TIME GENERALISATION[9]

Having considered the case of one-year term insurance within a discrete-time framework, we shall now generalise the analysis in two directions by considering insurance policies effective for periods of time greater than one year within a *continuous*-time framework. An immediate consequence of this generalisation is that it becomes possible in principle to analyse the optimal expenditure on a policy of *any* type (whether term, whole-life or endowment) for *any* configuration of premium payments.

Suppose, then, that at time $t = 0$ an individual's subjective probability density function for the time of his own death is $\rho(t)$. If the latest date at which the individual conceives it possible that he will still be alive is $t = T$ then $\rho(t)$ is defined on the interval $0 \leqslant t \leqslant T$. It will be assumed that $\rho(t)$ is continuous. Now in a continuous-time context specification of a consequence requires information concerning (a) the level of initial wealth[10] *and* (b) the time of death.

The continuous-time counterpart of the functions $L(w)$ and $D(w)$ of previous sections is therefore a utility function $U(w, t)$, defined on the set of ordered pairs

$$\{(w, t)|w \epsilon R, 0 \leqslant t \leqslant T\}$$

Thus $U(w, \bar{t})$ may be thought of as a utility of initial wealth function conditional on death at time $\bar{t}$.[11] It will be assumed that $U(w, t)$ is at least twice-differentiable with respect to both arguments and that

$$\frac{\partial U}{\partial w} > 0 \tag{4.30}$$

$$\frac{\partial U}{\partial t} > 0 \tag{4.31}$$

and

$$\frac{\partial^2 U}{\partial w^2} < 0. \tag{4.32}$$

(Equation (4.30) embodies the assumption that the individual prefers more initial wealth to less, (4.31) that he prefers to die later rather than sooner and (4.32) that he is financially risk-averse.)

If the individual has no uncertainty concerning his initial wealth, $\bar{w}$, then his expected utility is given by

$$E(U) = \int_0^T U(\bar{w}, t)\rho(t) \, dt. \tag{4.33}$$

Now suppose that the individual is offered the opportunity to purchase life insurance. If the individual does so then his initial wealth *itself* becomes contingent upon the time of death since the later the individual dies during the term of any insurance contract the later will the sum assured accrue to his estate[12] and hence the lower the discounted present value of the latter. For example, suppose that at $t = 0$ the individual plans to pay a premium x at time t_1 for insurance giving a sum assured, y, for a term from t_1 to t_2. The individual's wealth conditional on death at time t, denoted by w_t, is then given by

$$\left. \begin{aligned} w_t &= \bar{w}, \, (0 \leqslant t < t_1) \\ w_t &= \bar{w} - xe^{-it_1} + ye^{-it}, \, (t_1 \leqslant t \leqslant t_2) \\ w_t &= \bar{w} - xe^{-it_1}, \, (t_2 < t \leqslant T) \end{aligned} \right\} \tag{4.34}$$

where i is the appropriate[13] (continuous) discount rate, assumed to be independent of t.

For term insurance covering the period from t_1 to t_2, the graph of w_t will therefore be of the general form illustrated in figure 4.3.[14]

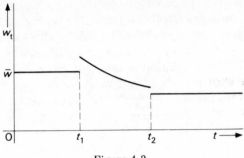

Figure 4.3.

Furthermore, for term insurance the 'fair/more than fair/less than fair' categorisation becomes

Fair insurance:
$$x = \int_{t_1}^{t_2} y e^{-i(t-t_1)} \frac{\rho(t)}{1 - F(t_1)} \, dt$$

More than fair insurance:
$$x < \int_{t_1}^{t_2} y e^{-i(t-t_1)} \frac{\rho(t)}{1 - F(t_1)} \, dt \qquad (4.35)$$

Less than fair insurance:
$$x > \int_{t_1}^{t_2} y e^{-i(t-t_1)} \frac{\rho(t)}{1 - F(t_1)} \, dt$$

where $F(t)$ is the distribution function corresponding to $\rho(t)$.

It follows from (4.34) that, for the particular term insurance under discussion,

$$\int_0^T w_t \rho(t) dt = \int_0^{t_1} \bar{w} \rho(t) dt + \int_{t_1}^{t_2} (\bar{w} - x e^{-it_1} + y e^{-it}) \rho(t) dt$$

$$+ \int_{t_2}^T (\bar{w} - x e^{-it_1}) \rho(t) dt \qquad (4.36)$$

$$= \bar{w} - x e^{-it_1} [1 - F(t_1)] + \int_{t_1}^{t_2} y e^{-it} \rho(t) dt. \qquad (4.37)$$

Thus, if insurance is fair, then from (4.35) and (4.37),

$$\int_0^T w_t \rho(t) dt = \bar{w} \qquad (4.38)$$

or, denoting $w_t - \bar{w}$ by δw_t,

$$\int_0^T \delta w_t \rho(t) dt = 0. \qquad (4.39)$$

So far we have considered a situation in which the individual plans to enter into only *one* term insurance for the period t_1 to t_2. However it is clear that, by replication of the above argument, (4.39) will hold for *any* fair term insurance and will therefore hold for the *aggregate* of fair term insurance held by the individual. Similarly, (4.39) could be shown to hold not only for fair *term* insurance but for fair *endowment* and *whole-life* insurance and consequently for the aggregate of all fair insurance (of whatever type) held by the individual.

Thus, if the aggregate effect of all life insurance held by the individual is to make $w_t = \bar{w} + \Delta w_t$ (so that Δw_t denotes the aggregate of δw_t) then, provided all insurance is fair, we can write

$$\int_0^T \Delta w_t \rho(t)dt = 0. \tag{4.40}$$

Given fair insurance opportunities, the individual's optimal planned time path of insurance expenditures will then be such as to maximise $E(U)$ *subject to (4.40)* where

$$E(U) = \int_0^T U(w_t, t)\rho(t)dt. \tag{4.41}$$

Strictly speaking it is also necessary to impose the condition

$$w_t \geqslant 0 \tag{4.42}$$

but it will be assumed that this constraint is never binding and can therefore be ignored.

Now suppose that

$$\frac{\partial^2 U}{\partial w \partial t}\bigg|_{w_t = \bar{w}} < 0. \tag{4.43}$$

If the individual plans to purchase some fair life insurance — say a whole-life policy — then the linear part of the increment in $E(U)$ due to this insurance is given by

$$\delta E(U) = \int_0^T \frac{\partial U}{\partial w} \delta w_t \rho(t)dt \tag{4.44}$$

where the variations δw_t will satisfy (4.39) and will in addition be strictly decreasing with time.

By choosing a sufficiently small planned expenditure on insurance it will be possible, in virtue of (4.43), to ensure that

$$\frac{d}{dt}\left(\frac{\partial U}{\partial w}\right) < 0. \tag{4.45}$$

From (4.39), (4.44) and (4.45) it then follows that we shall have $\delta E(U) > 0$, and (4.43) is therefore a *sufficient* condition for the purchase of some fair life insurance.

By contrast, suppose that (4.43) does *not* hold and consider any arbitrary planned time-path of life insurance expenditures. Suppose that this involves n policies, the nth being the latest planned purchase at time t_n. If the individual then considers a small reduction in his planned expenditure on the nth policy the linear part of the increment in $E(U)$ due to this reduction will be given by

$$\delta E(U) = \int_{t_n}^{T} \frac{\partial U}{\partial w} \, \delta w_t \rho(t) dt. \tag{4.46}$$

where the variations δw_t (being due solely to the reduction in planned expenditure on the nth policy) will be non-decreasing everywhere in the interval $[t_n, T]$ and *strictly increasing* somewhere in that interval and will also satisfy (4.39) so that

$$\int_{t_n}^{T} \delta w_t \rho(t) dt = 0. \tag{4.47}$$

In addition, because we are considering the purchase (rather than sale) of life insurance, w_t will be non-increasing in this interval so that if (4.43) does not hold then from (4.32)

$$\frac{d}{dt} \left(\frac{\partial U}{\partial w} \right) \geq 0, \, (t_n \leq t \leq T) \tag{4.48}$$

with a strong inequality somewhere in the interval.

From (4.46), (4.47) and (4.48) it follows that $\delta E(U) > 0$ and it is clear that the individual will wish to effect the reduction in planned expenditure on the nth policy. However, this argument will also apply to further reductions in expenditure on the nth policy and hence implies that the individual will prefer to *eliminate* the nth policy. Similarly with the $(n-1)th$ policy, the $(n-2)th$ policy and so on and it follows that if (4.43) fails to hold the individual will not plan to purchase *any* fair life insurance. (4.43) is thus not only a sufficient condition for the planned purchase of life insurance but is also *necessary*.

Finally, suppose that (4.43) applies. It is clear that the individual will then plan to purchase insurance up to the point at which *either* (4.42) is binding *or* $\partial U/\partial w$ becomes independent of the time of death, that is

$$\frac{d}{dt} \left(\frac{\partial U}{\partial w} \bigg|_{w_t \neq \bar{w}} \right) = 0. \tag{4.49}$$

Since the possibility that (4.42) is binding will be ignored in what follows, (4.49) will be taken to hold for any individual who purchases fair life insurance.

So far the analysis of the continuous time case has been almost exclusively concerned with *fair* life insurance. However, results for more than and less than fair life insurance can be derived by a virtually identical process of argument after appropriate weakening or strengthening of (4.39) to give

$$\int_0^T \delta w_t \rho(t)dt = \lambda. \tag{4.50}$$

where $\lambda > 0$ for more than fair insurance and $\lambda < 0$ for less than fair insurance.

The analysis of the continuous time case has therefore generated a set of results that have very obvious counterparts in the discrete time results derived in sections I—III. However, the one aspect of the earlier analysis that appears to have *no* natural extension in continuous time is the case of the individual whose indifference to the welfare of others is reflected in constancy of dD/dw.

V   IS INSURANCE FAIR?

It follows from the Central Limit Theorem[15] that the larger the number of life insurance contracts of a particular type[16] underwritten by an insurance company, the smaller the probability that the average payout per contract will diverge from the mathematical expectation of payout by more than a given amount.[17] Provided, then, that an insurance company does in fact underwrite a large number of contracts for each type of insurance that it sells, then the aggregate sum that it pays out in claims on any type of insurance will differ negligibly from the aggregate of expected[18] payouts per contract. Restricting attention to the simple single-period term insurance discussed in sections I to III, there is therefore little error in expressing the ith company's aggregate payout, c_{ij}, on insurance for individuals having probability p_j of death this period as

$$c_{ij} = p_j \sum_h y_{hij} \tag{4.51}$$

where y_{hij} is the amount of the ith company's one-period term insurance purchased by the hth member of that subset of the population comprising individuals having probability p_j of death this period.

The ith insurance company's profit, r_{ij}, on this class[19] of insurance is therefore given by

$$r_{ij} = \sum_h x_{h\,ij} - p_j \sum_h y_{h\,ij} - a_{ij} \qquad (4.52)$$

where $x_{h\,ij}$ is the premium payed to the ith company by the hth member of that subset of the population comprising individuals having probability p_j of death this period and a_{ij} is the total cost incurred by the ith company in administering this insurance.

With slight rearrangement (4.52) becomes

$$r_{ij} = (1 - p_j) \sum_h x_{h\,ij} - p_j \sum_h (y_{h\,ij} - x_{h\,ij}) - a_{ij}$$

so that, defining $z_{h\,ij}$ by

$$z_{ij} = y_{h\,ij} - x_{h\,ij} \qquad (4.53)$$

(4.52) may be written as

$$r_{ij} = (1 - p_j) \sum_h x_{h\,ij} - p_j \sum_h z_{h\,ij} - a_{ij}. \qquad (4.54)$$

Thus if (as before) it is assumed that

$$z_{h\,ij} = k_{ij} x_{h\,ij} \qquad (4.55)$$

then (4.54) becomes

$$r_{ij} = (1 - p_j) \sum_h x_{h\,ij} - p_j k_{ij} \sum_h x_{h\,ij} - a_{ij} \qquad (4.56)$$

so that, given positive administrative costs,

$$r_{ij} > 0 \Rightarrow k_{ij} < \frac{1 - p_j}{p_j}. \qquad (4.57)$$

Thus if this class of insurance is to make any contribution to the ith company's overall profit then *it must be less than fair*. Furthermore it is clear that the extent of the unfairness of the insurance will depend upon

(a) the magnitude of administrative costs; and
(b) the degree of competition in the market for this class of insurance.

However, the discussion thus far has ignored the tax treatment of life insurance premia. In the UK, for example, 50 per cent of life insurance premia are (up to a certain limit) deductible in the computation of taxable income. This means that for any individual paying income tax at marginal rate t_h the *net of tax* insurance premium is given by $x_{ijh}(1 - \tfrac{1}{2}t_h)$. The condition for insurance to be fair *from the point of view of the insured* is then

$$\frac{k_{ij}}{(1 - \tfrac{1}{2}t_h)} = \frac{1 - p_j}{p_j} . \tag{4.58}$$

Equations (4.57) and (4.58) therefore show that, while an insurance company *must* offer less than fair insurance in order to cover administrative costs and earn a profit, it is nonetheless quite conceivable that, owing to the tax treatment of insurance premia, such insurance may be *fair or even more than fair* from the point of view of the insured (i.e. net of tax).

The question of whether insurance is or is not fair net of tax is essentially one of fact and in an attempt to resolve this question the premium per pound sterling of gross sum assured, $1/(1 + k_j)$, at each age was regressed on probability of death, p_j, at the corresponding age using the premia quoted for one-year term insurance by a major British assurance company and probabilities of death derived from the appropriate mortality functions[20] in '*A 1949—52' Tables for Assured Lives Vol. 1*. The parameters of the regression relationship were estimated by least squares and the following results were obtained:

$$\frac{1}{1 + k_j} = \hat{\alpha} + \underset{(0.014)}{0.929\, p_j} + \hat{\epsilon}_j \qquad (R^2 = 0.997) \tag{4.59}$$

where $\hat{\alpha}$ depends upon the magnitude of the sum assured as shown in the table below:

$y_{hj}(\pounds)$	0—2000	2000—5000	5000—10,000	10,000—20,000
$\hat{\alpha}$	0.0020	0.0012	0.0006	0.0002

Thus, for example, an individual paying tax at the standard rate and purchasing between £5000 and £10,000 worth of one-year term insurance from this company will have

$$\frac{k_j}{1 - \tfrac{1}{2}t_h} = \frac{1.195 - 1.113\, p_j}{0.0006 + 0.929\, p_j} . \tag{4.60}$$

Furthermore

$$p_j \gtrless 0.002 \Rightarrow \frac{1.195 \ -1.113\,p_j}{0.0006+0.929\,p_j} \gtrless \frac{1-p_j}{p_j}\ . \qquad (4.61)$$

So that there would seem to be little error in treating this class of insurance as approximately fair from the point of view of the insured[21] (according to '*A 1949—52*' *Tables for Assured Lives Vol. 1*, p_j = 0.002 for males aged about forty-five, and so at this age such insurance will be *exactly* fair net of tax).

NOTES

1. *Assurance* is the earlier term, used alike of marine and life insurance before the end of the 16th c. Its general application is retained in the titles and policies of some long-established companies (e.g. the London Assurance Corporation). *Insurance* (in 17th c. also ENSURANCE) occurs first in reference to fire, but soon became co-extensive with *assurance*, the two terms being synonymous in Magens 1755. *Assurance* would probably have dropped out of use (as it has almost done in US), but that Babbage in 1826 proposed to restrict *insurance* to risks to property, and *assurance* to life insurance. This has been followed so far that *assurance* is now rarely used of marine, fire, or accident insurance, and is retained in Great Britain in the nomenclature and use of the majority of life insurance companies. But in general popular use, *insurance* is the prevalent term. [*Oxford English Dictionary* Vol. 5 p. 363]

   Throughout this book we shall refer to life *insurance*.

2. For the purposes of the analysis in this and later chapters, an individual's wealth at time t is defined as the market value of the individual's *marketable* assets (less his liabilities) at time t. The reason for excluding non-marketable assets (such as human wealth in the form of anticipated future labour income) is that wealth will be treated as the upper bound to the amount that can be spent on life insurance, or forfeited to effect risk reduction, and inclusion of non-marketable assets would clearly overstate this upper bound. To the extent that human wealth *is* marketable, the magnitude of current wealth will itself depend upon whether or not the individual survives the current period. If this is the case it will be necessary to include in the definition of wealth specification of whether the magnitude of wealth is conditional on survival or death (i.e., it will be meaningless to assert that an individual's current wealth is $\bar{w}$ without specifying whether or not it has been assumed that the individual will survive the current period, thereby preserving the marketable component of human wealth). In order to avoid the latter complication it will be assumed that the amount of marketable human wealth is sufficiently small in relation to other marketable assets to be neglected.

3. This is essentially the same formulation of the optimal life insurance problem as the one adopted by Eisner and Strotz (1961), Drèze (1962) and Parkin and Wu (1972). Fortune (1973) also considers the optimal expenditure on life insurance from an expected utility-maximising point of view but fails to recognise the importance of the *conditional* utility approach.

4. An individual is said to display 'risk aversion' if he is unwilling to accept a gamble whose mathematical expectation of gain is less than or equal to zero. It is fairly easy to show that risk aversion is equivalent to strict concavity of the utility of wealth function.

5. For an account of the St Petersburg Paradox see, for example, Ozga (1965) pp. 171–3.

6. Briefly, unless $L(w)$ is bounded above then it is possible to construct a game involving a finite gain $G(n)$ — where n is the number of times it is necessary to toss a coin before 'tails' comes up — such that an individual will pay an infinite sum to participate in the game as the potential recipient of the sum $G(n)$. Conversely, unless $D(w)$ is bounded below it is possible to construct a similar game involving gains $\overline{G}(n)$ such that it would require an infinite sum to induce an individual to participate in the game as the person who *pays out* $\overline{G}(n)$.

7. Recall that, by assumption, $0 < \bar{p} < 1$.

8. See, for example, Friedman and Savage (1948).

9. Two other analyses dealing with the question of optimal life insurance in an extended time context are Yaari (1965) and Fischer (1973). Both analyses adopt the 'expected utility-maximisation' hypothesis and seek to establish, in particular, the properties of an optimal planned time-path of consumption in a situation in which life insurance can be purchased. Because these analyses are intimately concerned with optimal lifetime consumption streams (and in addition are based upon fairly specific assumptions concerning the form of utility functions defined on the set of such consumption streams) they are not particularly suitable analytical devices for the derivation of the kind of conditions with which we are concerned in the present chapter.

10. See n. 2. Also notice that at the most general level initial wealth will *itself* depend in part upon the time of death ((a) because the magnitude of an individual's human wealth depends upon the length of his working life, and (b) because the discounted present value of insurance payoffs depends upon the time of death). However, our earlier definition of wealth as the market value of *marketable* assets (less liabilities) requires that non-marketable assets (including the bulk of an individual's human wealth) be excluded in the determination of the level of an individual's wealth for present purposes. For this reason an *uninsured* individual's wealth is regarded as parametric and independent of the time of death whereas an *insured* individual's wealth is treated as non-parametric. (There would of course be little difficulty in treating weath as quite generally dependent upon the time of death — it simply seems analytically convenient and empirically justifiable to ignore the dependence in the absence of life insurance.)

11. If the current period ends at $t = \tau$ then the functions $L(w)$ and $D(w)$ of the previous analysis may be regarded as a discontinuous version of $U(w, t)$ as follows:

$$U(w, t) \equiv L(w) \quad (\tau < t)$$
$$U(w, t) \equiv D(w) \quad (0 \leqslant t \leqslant \tau).$$

12. Notice that, since the insured can nominate anyone as his beneficiary in the insurance contract, the market value of marketable assets (less liabilities) *contingent on death at time t* will legitimately include the present value of any sum assured on the death of the insured at time t. That is, if it is known for certain that the insured will die at $t = \bar{t}$ then nomination as the beneficiary in an insurance contract is presumably worth the present value of the sum assured and will therefore command a market value equal to this present value.

13. This will presumably depend in part upon the degree of confidence that people have in the soundness of the particular insurance company.

14. Assuming that $i > 0$ and $y > x$.

15. In essence the Central Limit Theorem asserts: 'The mean, $\bar{x}$, of a sample of n identically but independently distributed random variables, each with mean μ and variance σ^2 is itself asymptotically normal with mean μ and variance σ^2/n.' For a proof of this theorem see, for example, Hogg and Craig (1965).

16. Given that the Central Limit Theorem applies to a sample of n *identically* distributed random variables, a 'type' of life insurance in this context must strictly speaking be an insurance for a *particular* sum assured, a *particular* term and a *particular* risk at each date within the term (i.e. £3000 worth of one-year term insurance for a twenty-eight-year-old male in good health). It is also necessary to assume statistical independence between the payoffs on each individual insurance of any particular type.

17. This is an immediate consequence of the Central Limit Theorem, which implies that the variance of the average payout will be a *decreasing* function of the number of contracts underwritten. Notice also that since life insurance premia are computed largely on the basis of mortality statistics, a 'relative frequency' interpretation of the concept of probability seems appropriate in the current context.

18. Here the term 'expected' is used in the formal sense of a 'mathematical expectation'.

19. A 'class' of insurance includes all life-insurance contracts of a given term and risk irrespective of the amount insured.

20. Since the analysis is concerned with one-year term insurance, it seemed appropriate to use the so-called 'select' functions $l_{[x]}$ and $d_{[x]}$ in computing probabilities of death at various ages. In essence, select mortality functions relate mortality to age for that section of the population *excluding* obviously infirm individuals. Insurance companies employ select mortality functions in establishing the premia for *short*-term insurance since the likelihood of correctly predicting infirmity at age x (and applying an

appropriate loading to the premium) is greatly enhanced if the individual can be medically examined shortly beforehand, as will be possible with short-term insurance.

21. Strictly speaking, this proposition is true only if the insured's *subjective* probability for his own death during a particular period coincides with the *objective* probability which the insurance company deduces from mortality statistics. However, it does not seem unreasonable to assume that such correspondence normally occurs to an adequate degree of approximation.

REFERENCES

Drèze, J. 'L'Utilité Sociale d'une Vie Humaine', *Revue Française de Recherche Operationelle* (1962)

Eisner, R. and Strotz, R. H. 'Flight Insurance and the Theory of Choice', *Journal of Political Economy* (August 1961)

Fischer, S. 'A Life Cycle Model of Life Insurance Purchases' *International Economic Review* (February 1973)

Fortune, P. 'A Theory of Optimal Life Insurance: Development and Tests' *Journal of Finance* (June 1973)

Friedman, M. and Savage, L. J. 'The Utility Analysis of Choices Involving Risk' *Journal of Political Economy* (August 1948)

Hogg, R. V. and Craig, A. T. *Introduction to Mathematical Statistics* London, Collier Macmillan (1965)

Ozga, S. A. *Expectations in Economic Theory* London, Weidenfeld and Nicolson (1965)

Parkin, J. M. and Wu, S. Y. 'Choice Involving Unwanted Risky Events and Optimal Insurance' *American Economic Review* (December 1972)

Yaari, M. E. 'Uncertain Lifetime, Life Insurance and the Theory of the Consumer' *Review of Economic Studies* (April 1965)

5. The Value of Changes in Safety and Longevity: Theory[1]

This chapter will be primarily concerned with the derivation of a set of *qualitative* results concerning an individual's valuation (in the form of compensating variations in wealth[2]) of changes in the (subjective) probability of his own death. Some attention will also be given to the value placed by the individual upon (a) changes in the probability of his own involvement in a non-fatal accident and (b) changes in the probability of death or non-fatal accident for anyone else. The value of avoidance of real resource costs and net output losses will, however, *not* be discussed, the theoretical and empirical analysis of these questions having been considered in some detail elsewhere.[3] Finally, for the sake of completeness we shall examine the relationship between compensating and *equivalent*[4] variations in wealth for changes in safety.

The analysis will be developed within the same basic framework as was employed in examining optimal expenditures on life insurance in the previous chapter — that is, it will be assumed throughout that it is legitimate to treat the individual under consideration as an expected utility-maximiser — and the analysis will again be conducted first within a single-period, discrete-time context and subsequently generalised as far as possible to a continuous-time basis. In addition the functions $L(w)$, $D(w)$ and $U(w, t)$ will be assumed to possess the properties specified in sections II and IV of the preceding chapter. Finally, following the discussion of section 4.V, it will be assumed that, in view of the tax treatment of life insurance premia, this type of insurance is approximately fair from the point of view of the insured and that there is therefore negligible error in treating such insurance as if it is, in fact, *precisely* fair. The analysis of sections 4.II and 4.III then indicates that, in the single-period case for example, we need consider just *two* alternative sets of restrictions on $L(w)$ and $D(w)$:

either individual does not purchase life insurance, so that from (4.26)

$$\frac{dL}{dw}\bigg|_{w=\bar{w}} \geq \frac{dD}{dw}\bigg|_{w=\bar{w}} \tag{5.1}$$

or individual purchases life insurance, so that from (4.9)

$$(\bar{w} - x)\left(\frac{dL}{dw}\bigg|_{w=\bar{w}-x} - \frac{dD}{dw}\bigg|_{w=\bar{w}+z}\right) = 0. \tag{5.2}$$

Similarly, in the continuous-time case the assumption that insurance is fair after tax will allow us to limit our attention to just two alternative sets of restrictions on $U(w, t)$.

I THE SINGLE-PERIOD CASE: INDIVIDUAL UNINSURED

As in the previous chapter we shall begin by considering a single-period, discrete-time problem in which the individual is assumed not to distinguish between the various instants of time within the period under analysis. Suppose, then, that the individual begins the current period with wealth $\bar{w}$ and associates a subjective probability $\bar{p}(0 < \bar{p} < 1)$ with the outcome of his own death during this period. His initial expected utility is then given by

$$E(U) = (1 - \bar{p})L(\bar{w}) + \bar{p}D(\bar{w}) \tag{5.3}$$

where $L(w)$ and $D(w)$ are, as previously defined, utility of wealth functions conditional on survival and death during the current period, respectively.

Now suppose that the individual is offered the opportunity to reduce the probability of his death during the current period from $\bar{p}$ to $p(<\bar{p})$. Given the restrictions on $L(w)$ and $D(w)$ embodied in (4.10), (4.12) and (4.14), the individual will be prepared to *forfeit* wealth in order to effect this improvement in his safety. Furthermore the *maximum* sum, v, that he will forfeit must be such as to leave him with the same level of expected utility as in the initial situation. v must therefore satisfy the following condition:[5]

$$(1 - p)L(\bar{w} - v) + pD(\bar{w} - v) = (1 - \bar{p})L(\bar{w}) + \bar{p}D(\bar{w}). \tag{5.4}$$

Similarly, if the individual is to be induced to accept an *increase* in probability then the *minimum* sum he will accept as compensation will increase his wealth to a level such that the augmented probability and wealth also satisfy equation (5.4).[6]

Clearly, then, v — as defined by equation (5.4) — is the individual's compensating variation in wealth for a change in the subjective probability of his own death from $\bar{p}$ to any other level, p. Following the discussion in chapters 1 and 2, it is therefore a matter of some interest to establish the general properties of the functional relationship, $v(p)$, between v and p implied by equation (5.4). Since this will involve examination of a number of complicated expressions it will be convenient to introduce some notational simplification. In the rest of this chapter we shall therefore employ the following definitions:

$$L \equiv L(\bar{w} - v)$$

$$D \equiv D(\bar{w} - v)$$

$$L' \equiv \frac{\partial L(\bar{w} - v)}{\partial v}$$

$$D' \equiv \frac{\partial D(\bar{w} - v)}{\partial v}$$

$$L'' \equiv \frac{\partial^2 L(\bar{w} - v)}{\partial v^2}$$

$$D'' \equiv \frac{\partial^2 D(\bar{w} - v)}{\partial v^2} .$$

Finally, since p is a probability it is immediate that $v(p)$ is defined only on the closed interval $0 \leqslant p \leqslant 1$.

Differentiating through (5.4) and rearranging we get

$$\frac{\partial v}{\partial p} = \frac{L - D}{(1 - p)L' + pD'} . \tag{5.5}$$

It then follows that

$$\frac{\partial^2 v}{\partial p^2} = \frac{[(1-p)L' + pD'](L' - D')\dfrac{\partial v}{\partial p} . - (L-D)\left\{[(1-p)L'' + pD'']\dfrac{\partial v}{\partial p} + (D' - L')\right\}}{[(1-p)L' + pD']^2} \tag{5.6}$$

But from (4.10), (4.11), (4.12), (4.13) and (4.14) respectively,

$$L' < 0 \qquad (5.7)$$

$$L'' < 0 \qquad (5.8)$$

$$D' \leqslant 0 \qquad (5.9)$$

$$D'' \leqslant 0 \qquad (5.10)$$

and

$$L > D. \qquad (5.11)$$

Also, since we are considering the situation in which the individual does not purchase fair insurance, we know from (5.1) that

$$L' \leqslant D'. \qquad (5.12)$$

Thus, from (5.5) together with (5.7), (5.9) and (5.11)[7]

$$\frac{\partial v}{\partial p} < 0, \qquad (0 \leqslant p < 1) \qquad (5.13)$$

so that from (5.6) together with (5.7)—(5.13)

$$\frac{\partial^2 v}{\partial p^2} < 0, \qquad (0 \leqslant p < 1). \qquad (5.14)$$

The graph of $v(p)$ will therefore be of the general form depicted in figure 5.1.

Notice first that v is positive for values of p less than $\bar{p}$ since the individual will be prepared to *forfeit* wealth to effect improvements in safety. Conversely v is negative for values of p greater than $\bar{p}$ since the individual will require *compensation* for deterioration in his

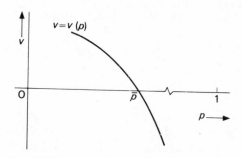

Figure 5.1.

safety. It should perhaps be emphasised that allocative decisions frequently will involve consideration of adverse as well as beneficial effects upon the safety of life so that the relationship between v and p for values of p exceeding $\bar{p}$ is of more than academic interest.

Having established the general form of the relationship between v and p, let us now consider three aspects of this relationship in greater detail. These three aspects are:

(a) the behaviour of $v(p)$ as p approaches zero;
(b) the behaviour of $v(p)$ as p approaches unity;
(c) the derivative $\partial v/\partial p$ evaluated at $p = \bar{p}$.

Clearly (a) and (b) will involve individual attitudes towards extremes of safety and danger and will therefore be relevant only for those investment programmes that have very pronounced effects upon the safety of life. However $-(\partial v/\partial p)$ evaluated at $p = \bar{p}$ is the marginal value of a decrease[8] in risk from the initial risk level and is therefore directly relevant for all investment programmes that have the effect of making life marginally safer (or riskier). Since investments having relatively small effects upon the safety of life are probably most common, it is clear that $\partial v/\partial p$ evaluated at $p = \bar{p}$ is of primary importance for policy purposes.

(a)   The behaviour of $v(p)$ as p approaches zero

Suppose that $L(w)$ is such that

$$L^{-1}[(1-\bar{p})\bar{L} + \bar{p}\bar{D}] > 0 \tag{5.15}$$

where $L^{-1}(U)$ is the inverse function[9] of $L(w)$, $\bar{L}$ denotes $L(w)$ evaluated at $w = \bar{w}$ and $\bar{D}$ denotes $D(w)$ evaluated at $w = \bar{w}$. In this case, setting $p = 0$ in (5.4) yields a value of v — say v_0 — such that

$$v_0 < \bar{w}. \tag{5.16}$$

If (5.15) holds, then, the individual will *not* be prepared to bankrupt himself to make life completely safe during the current period[10] and the graph of $v(p)$ will have an intercept $v_0(<\bar{w})$ on the v-axis.

If, by contrast, the inequality in (5.15) is reversed then the individual *will* be prepared to bankrupt himself in order to reduce the probability of death in the current period from $\bar{p}$ to some value $\tilde{p}$ such that

$$0 < \tilde{p} < \bar{p}. \tag{5.17}$$

In order to determine the behaviour of $v(p)$ for values of p between $\tilde{p}$ and zero it is necessary to establish whether or not the individual is able to borrow when bankrupt (i.e. when $w = 0$). If he is unable to do so then, as noted earlier,[11] v will be subject to the constraint

$$v \leqslant \bar{w}. \tag{5.18}$$

$v(p)$ will then be such that

$$0 \leqslant p \leqslant \tilde{p} \Rightarrow v(p) = \bar{w}. \tag{5.19}$$

The graph of $v(p)$ will therefore become horizontal for values of p less than or equal to $\tilde{p}$. Notice that since (5.5) and (5.6) apply only when (5.4) holds as a strict equality — which will *not* be the case for values of p less than or equal to $\tilde{p}$ — there is no inconsistency between (5.13) (5.14) and (5.19).

If bankruptcy imposes no constraint on borrowing then v will continue to increase as p is reduced below $\tilde{p}$. The graph of $v(p)$ will then have an intercept v_0' on the v-axis such that

$$v_0' > \bar{w}. \tag{5.20}$$

Finally, suppose that

$$L^{-1}[(1 - \bar{p})\bar{L} + \bar{p}\bar{D}] = 0. \tag{5.21}$$

In this case the individual will not bankrupt himself for anything other than the complete elimination of the risk of death during the current period. The graph of $v(p)$ will therefore have an intercept v_0'' on the v-axis such that

$$v_0'' = \bar{w}. \tag{5.22}$$

(b)   *The behaviour of $v(p)$ as p approaches unity*

In section 4.II it was argued that if $L(w)$ is not bounded above then it is possible to construct a variant of the St Petersburg game such that the individual will be prepared to pay an indefinitely large sum to participate in the game. Since it is an observable fact that the majority of people will *not* pay indefinitely large stakes to participate in such games, it would seem necessary to regard $L(w)$ as bounded above. If this is so then by (5.11) $D(w)$ will also be bounded above. The least upper bound of $L(w)$ will be denoted by α and the least upper bound of $D(w)$ by β.[12] Suppose that

$$\beta > (1 - \bar{p})\bar{L} + \bar{p}\bar{D}. \tag{5.23}$$

It then follows that there exists a finite value of w that will make $D(w)$ equal to the initial level of expected utility. There must therefore exist a finite value of v that will satisfy equation (5.4) when $p = 1$, so that there exists a finite sum sufficient to compensate the individual for the certainty of death during the current period. In this case the graph of $v(p)$ will have a finite negative intercept on the line $p = 1$.

Conversely, suppose that

$$\beta \leqslant (1 - \bar{p})L + \bar{p}\bar{D}. \tag{5.24}$$

In this case, no finite sum will be sufficient to compensate the individual for the certainty of death. Furthermore, it follows from (4.10) and (5.4) that

$$\lim_{p \to p*} v = -\infty \tag{5.25}$$

where[13]

$$p* = \frac{\alpha - (1 - \bar{p})\bar{L} - \bar{p}\bar{D}}{\alpha - \beta}. \tag{5.26}$$

Notice that if (5.24) holds as a *strong* inequality then $p*$ will be strictly less than unity so that there will exist a *range* of probabilities of death (namely $p* \leqslant p \leqslant 1$) for which it will be impossible to compensate the individual.[14] The graph of $v(p)$ will then be asymptotic to the line $p = p*$.

(c)   *The derivative $\partial v/\partial p$ evaluated at $p = \bar{p}$*

When $p = \bar{p}$, it follows from (5.4) that $v = 0$. The derivative $\partial v/\partial p$ evaluated at $p = \bar{p}$, which will be denoted by $(\partial v/\partial p)_{\bar{p}}$, may therefore be obtained simply by setting $p = \bar{p}$ and $v = 0$ in (5.5), i.e.

$$\left(\frac{\partial v}{\partial p}\right)_{\bar{p}} = \frac{\bar{L} - \bar{D}}{(1 - \bar{p})\bar{L}' + \bar{p}\bar{D}'} \tag{5.27}$$

where $\bar{L}'$ denotes L' evaluated at $v = 0$ and $\bar{D}'$ denotes D' evaluated at $v = 0$.

Now let us consider the manner in which the marginal value of a decrease in risk, $-(\partial v/\partial p)_{\bar{p}}$, varies with initial risk, $\bar{p}$, and initial wealth, $\bar{w}$. Differentiating through (5.27) partially with respect to $\bar{p}$ gives

$$\frac{\partial \left(\frac{\partial v}{\partial p}\right)_{\bar{p}}}{\partial \bar{p}} = \frac{(\bar{D} - \bar{L})(\bar{D}' - \bar{L}')}{[(1 - \bar{p})\bar{L}' + \bar{p}\bar{D}']^2} \tag{5.28}$$

while differentiating through (5.27) partially with respect to $\bar{w}$ gives

$$\frac{\partial \left(\frac{\partial v}{\partial p}\right)_{\bar{p}}}{\partial \bar{w}} = \frac{[(1-\bar{p})\bar{L}' + \bar{p}\bar{D}']\,(\bar{D}'-\bar{L}') + (\bar{L}-\bar{D})\,[(1-\bar{p})\bar{L}'' + \bar{p}\bar{D}'']}{[(1-\bar{p})\bar{L}' + \bar{p}\bar{D}']^2}.$$

(5.29)

where $\bar{L}''$ denotes L'' evaluated at $v = 0$ and $\bar{D}''$ denotes D'' evaluated at $v = 0$. Thus, from (5.28) together with (5.11) and (5.12),

$$\frac{\partial \left(\frac{\partial v}{\partial p}\right)_{\bar{p}}}{\partial \bar{p}} \leqslant 0$$

(5.30)

while from (5.29) together with (5.7)—(5.12)

$$\frac{\partial \left(\frac{\partial v}{\partial p}\right)_{\bar{p}}}{\partial \bar{w}} < 0.$$

(5.31)

Notice first that (5.30) indicates that the marginal value of a decrease in risk from the initial risk level, $-(\partial v/\partial p)_{\bar{p}}$, is a *non-decreasing* function of initial risk. In fact, it follows from (5.28) that the marginal value of a decrease in risk from the initial risk level will be a strictly *increasing* function of initial risk wherever (5.12) holds as a strong inequality. Furthermore (5.31) shows that safety improvement is a *non-inferior* good for the type of individual under consideration.

It is important to remember, however, that the analysis so far has concentrated upon the type of individual who chooses not to purchase life insurance. We shall now proceed to consider the alternative situation in which the individual *does* purchase insurance, our prime concern being to establish whether or not the various results concerning the properties of $v(p)$ continue to hold.

II   THE SINGLE-PERIOD CASE: INDIVIDUAL INSURED

By an extension of the argument that led to equation (5.4), an individual who purchases life insurance will pay a maximum sum, v, to effect a safety improvement (in the form of a reduction in the subjective probability of his own death from $\bar{p}$ to $p(<\bar{p}))$ where v satisfies the following condition:[15]

$$(1-p)L(\bar{w}-v-x) + pD(\bar{w}-v+z) = (1-\bar{p})L(\bar{w}-\bar{x}) + \bar{p}D(\bar{w}+\bar{z})$$

(5.32)

where $\bar{x}$ denotes the optimal insurance premium[16] prior to the risk change,

x denotes the optimal insurance premium after the risk change,

$\bar{z}$ denotes the net sum assured prior to the risk change,

z denotes the net sum assured after the risk change, and all other variables are as previously defined.

Similarly, if the individual is to be induced to accpt an *increase* in risk then the minimum sum he will accept as compensation will, together with the increased probability of death, also satisfy (5.32).

It can then be shown that expressions for $\partial v/\partial p$ and $\partial^2 v/\partial p^2$ are given simply by replacing $L(\bar{w}-v)$ by $L(\bar{w}-v-x)$, $D(\bar{w}-v)$ by $D(\bar{w}-v+z)$ etc., in equations (5.5) and (5.6).[17] Thus, introducing the following definitions,

$$\Theta = L(\bar{w}-v-x)$$

$$\Psi = D(\bar{w}-v+z)$$

$$\Theta' = \frac{\partial L(\bar{w}-v-x)}{\partial v}$$

$$\Psi' = \frac{\partial D(\bar{w}-v+z)}{\partial v}$$

$$\Theta'' = \frac{\partial^2 L(\bar{w}-v-x)}{\partial v^2}$$

$$\Psi'' = \frac{\partial^2 D(\bar{w}-v+z)}{\partial v^2}$$

we have

$$\frac{\partial v}{\partial p} = \frac{\Theta - \Psi}{(1-p)\Theta' + p\Psi'}$$

(5.33)

and

$$\frac{\partial^2 v}{\partial p^2} = \frac{[(1-p)\Theta' + p\Psi'] (\Theta' - \Psi')\dfrac{\partial v}{\partial p} - (\Theta - \Psi)\left\{[(1-p)\Theta'' + p\Psi'']\dfrac{\partial v}{\partial p} + (\Psi' - \Theta')\right\}}{[(1-p)\Theta' + p\Psi']^2} .$$

(5.34)

But from (4.12), (4.13), (4.14) and (4.15) respectively

$$\Theta' < 0 \qquad (5.35)$$

$$\Theta'' < 0 \qquad (5.36)$$

$$\Psi' \leqslant 0 \qquad (5.37)$$

and

$$\Psi'' \leqslant 0. \qquad (5.38)$$

Furthermore, if insurance is fair and the individual purchases insurance in an amount less than his current wealth then, from (5.2) x and z will be chosen so as to ensure that[18]

$$\Theta' = \Psi'. \qquad (5.39)$$

Finally, it will be assumed that the chosen values of x and z are such that

$$\Theta > \Psi \qquad (5.40)$$

(that is, we shall ignore the bizarre possibility that the individual might, by purchasing sufficient life insurance, augment wealth contingent on death relative to wealth contingent on survival to such an extent that death becomes preferable to survival).

From (5.33) together with (5.35), (5.36) and (5.40) it follows that[19]

$$\frac{\partial v}{\partial p} < 0 \qquad (5.41)$$

so that from (5.34) together with (5.35)—(5.41)

$$\frac{\partial^2 v}{\partial p^2} < 0. \qquad (5.42)$$

Thus it is clear that the results established in section 5.I concerning the general form of $v(p)$ for the uninsured individual, *also* hold in a neighbourhood of $\bar{p}$ for an individual who buys (fair) life insurance. In a similar way it is possible to show that the more specific results established in section 5.I concerning the behaviour of $v(p)$ at extreme values of p and the derivative $(\partial v/\partial p)_{\bar{p}}$ also apply to the individual who buys insurance with the sole exception of (5.30) which becomes a strong equality; i.e.

$$\frac{\partial \left(\frac{\partial v}{\partial p} \right)_{\bar{p}}}{\partial \bar{p}} = 0. \qquad (5.43)$$

III   THE SINGLE-PERIOD CASE: SUMMARY

The analysis of sections 5.I and 5.II therefore indicates that *whether or not* the individual purchases (fair) life insurance $v(p)$ will be such that[20]

$$\frac{\partial v}{\partial p} < 0, \quad (0 \leqslant p < 1) \tag{5.44}$$

$$\frac{\partial^2 v}{\partial p^2} < 0, \quad (0 \leqslant p < 1). \tag{5.45}$$

In addition the behaviour of $v(p)$ for extreme values of p will be as shown in figure 5.2. Furthermore in both the insured and uninsured cases, the marginal value of a decrease in risk evaluated at the initial risk level is a *unambiguously increasing* function of initial wealth, i.e.

$$\frac{\partial - \left(\dfrac{\partial v}{\partial p}\right)_{\bar{p}}}{\partial \bar{w}} > 0. \tag{5.46}$$

It appears, therefore, that safety may be treated as a non-inferior good.

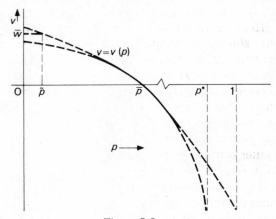

Figure 5.2.

Finally it has been demonstrated that the marginal value of a decrease in risk evaluated at the initial risk level is a non-decreasing function of initial risk, i.e.

$$\frac{\partial - \left(\dfrac{\partial v}{\partial p}\right)_{\bar{p}}}{\partial \bar{p}} \geqslant 0 \tag{5.47}$$

with the equality applying in *all* insured cases and in those uninsured cases for which (5.12) holds as an equality.

Equations (5.46) and (5.47) therefore indicate that a conventional cost—benefit analysis (narrowly conceived to eschew the evaluation of distributional effects) will tend to recommend the utilisation of scarce safety-improvement resources in *relatively* high-income, high-risk areas. Lest the first of these results be misinterpreted or adduced as evidence of the moral poverty of cost—benefit analysis, it must be stressed that a responsible social decision-maker would normally be expected to consider distributional effects *together with* the results of a cost—benefit analysis and not to base allocative decisions on the latter alone.[21]

IV   THE CONTINUOUS-TIME CASE: INDIVIDUAL UNINSURED

So far the analysis in this chapter has been developed within a single-period, discrete-time framework. While this has made for analytical simplicity, it has also imposed two rather severe restrictions on the generality of the discussion. In the first place it has not been possible to consider the type of change in safety that is expected to affect mortality and accident rates during an *extended* time horizon: since the majority of safety improvements are presumably of this nature, this is clearly a rather serious defect. The second limitation of the preceding analysis is that it has not been possible to draw any distinction between the various instants within the time period under consideration and this in turn has made it impossible to recognise that if an individual is to die during a particular time period then he will (presumably) prefer to do so later rather than sooner during the period.

Both of these limitations disappear, however, when the analysis is conducted in a continuous-time context: the restriction on the time horizon is removed and it also becomes possible to talk of death at a particular *point of time*, thereby eliminating the temporal ambiguity of the concept of death 'during the tth period'. The price of this gain in generality is unfortunately a marked increase in the severity of the analysis from a purely technical point of view.

Following the discussion in section 4.IV we shall write the individual's initial expected utility as

$$E(U) = \int_0^T U(\bar{w}, t)\bar{\rho}(t)dt \qquad (5.48)$$

where $\bar{w}$ denotes initial wealth,

t denotes time of death,

$U(w, t)$ is a utility function (of the type discussed in section 4.IV) whose arguments are initial wealth and time of death,

$\bar{\rho}(t)$ is the initial (by assumption, continuous and unimodal) subjective probability density function for time of death, and

T is the latest time at which the individual conceives it possible that he may still be alive.

By a similar argument to that adduced in obtaining equation (5.4), the maximum sum, v, that the individual would forfeit (or the minimum sum he would accept as compensation) for swopping the probability density function $\bar{\rho}(t)$ for some other density function $\rho(t)$ would then satisfy[22]

$$\int_0^T U(\bar{w} - v, t)\rho(t)dt = \int_0^T U(\bar{w}, t)\bar{\rho}(t)dt. \tag{5.49}$$

The important question is then the relationship between $\rho(t)$ and $\bar{\rho}(t)$. While it is possible to imagine a wide variety of alternative ways in which an expenditure on safety improvement might affect the probability density function for time of death, it is not at all clear which general type of effect might be sufficiently predominant to warrant detailed investigation. At first sight it might seem most natural to begin by considering the value of the type of safety improvement whose sole effect is to increase the *mean* of $\bar{\rho}(t)$, leaving all other parameters of the distribution unaffected (this might be referred to as a pure increase in life expectancy). Unfortunately, for essentially technical reasons it will be possible to perturb $\bar{\rho}(t)$ by a *strictly ceteris paribus* variation in mean only in rather exceptional circumstances.[23] That is, the typical safety change will involve replacement of $\bar{\rho}(t)$ by a density function differing from $\bar{\rho}(t)$ in more than just mean. None the less, it seems likely that in a significant proportion of cases the variation in mean of $\bar{\rho}(t)$ will dominate the variation in other parameters to such an extent that the perturbation of $\bar{\rho}(t)$ can be adequately *approximated* by a change in mean alone. Accordingly, we shall proceed to consider those safety improvements that are assumed to affect only the mean of $\bar{\rho}(t)$, or in less formal terms those whose sole effect is to increase (or decrease) life expectancy.

As in section 5.I, it will be useful to begin by introducing some notational simplification in the form of the following definitions:

$$U \equiv U(\bar{w} - v, t)$$

$$U_v \equiv \frac{\partial U(\bar{w} - v, t)}{\partial v}$$

$$U_{vv} \equiv \frac{\partial^2 U(\bar{w} - v, t)}{\partial v^2}$$

$$U_{vt} \equiv \frac{\partial^2 U(\bar{w} - v, t)}{\partial v \, \partial t}.$$

Differentiating through (5.49) with respect to μ and rearranging gives

$$\frac{\partial v}{\partial \mu} = \frac{-\int_0^T U \frac{\partial \rho}{\partial \mu} \, dt}{\int_0^T \rho(t) U_v \, dt}. \tag{5.50}$$

It then follows that

$$\frac{\partial^2 v}{\partial \mu^2} = \frac{-\left[\int_0^T \rho(t) U_v dt\right] \left[\int_0^T \left(U \frac{\partial^2 \rho}{\partial \mu^2} + U_v \frac{\partial v}{\partial \mu} \frac{\partial \rho}{\partial \mu}\right) dt\right] + \left(\int_0^T U \frac{\partial \rho}{\partial \mu} \, dt\right) \left\{\int_0^T \left[U_v \frac{\partial \rho}{\partial \mu} + \rho(t) U_{vv} \frac{\partial v}{\partial \mu}\right] dt\right\}}{\left(\int_0^T \rho(t) U_v dt\right)^2}. \tag{5.51}$$

In order to establish the signs of $\partial v/\partial \mu$ and $\partial^2 v/\partial \mu^2$ it will be necessary to examine the signs of the various integrals in (5.50) and (5.51).

From (4.30) $U_v < 0$. Also, $\rho(t) \geqslant 0$ (with $\rho(t) > 0$ for some $0 < t < T$) so that

$$\int_0^T \rho(t) U_v dt < 0. \tag{5.52}$$

Furthermore, both (5.50) and (5.51) contain integrals of the following form:

$$\int_0^T f(t) \frac{\partial \rho}{\partial \mu} \, dt. \tag{5.53}$$

But, by the definition of $\rho(t)$,

$$\int_0^T \frac{\partial \rho}{\partial \mu} \, dt = \frac{\partial}{\partial \mu} \int_0^T \rho(t) dt = 0 \qquad (5.54)$$

and for $\rho(t)$ unimodal (which it is assumed to be) with mode at t_m

$$\left.\begin{array}{l} 0 \leqslant t < t_m \Rightarrow \dfrac{\partial \rho}{\partial \mu} < 0 \\[2ex] t_m < t \leqslant T \Rightarrow \dfrac{\partial \rho}{\partial \mu} > 0 \end{array}\right\} \qquad (5.55)$$

so that from (5.54) and (5.55)

$$f'(t) \gtrless 0 \Rightarrow \int_0^T f(t) \frac{\partial \rho}{\partial \mu} \, dt \gtrless 0. \qquad (5.56)$$

Thus, from (4.31) and (5.56),

$$\int_0^T U \frac{\partial \rho}{\partial \mu} \, dt > 0. \qquad (5.57)$$

Hence from (5.50) together with (5.52) and (5.57),

$$\frac{\partial v}{\partial \mu} > 0. \qquad (5.58)$$

From (4.32) and (5.58), it then follows that

$$\int_0^T \rho(t) U_{vv} \frac{\partial v}{\partial \mu} \, dt < 0. \qquad (5.59)$$

Since we are considering the case in which no (fair) life insurance is held, (4.43) cannot hold, so that

$$\frac{\partial U_v}{\partial t} \leqslant 0. \qquad (5.60)$$

Thus from (5.56) and (5.60),

$$\int_0^T U_v \frac{\partial \rho}{\partial \mu} \, dt \leqslant 0, \qquad (5.61)$$

and from (5.56), (5.58) and (5.60)

$$\int_0^T U_v \frac{\partial v}{\partial \rho} \frac{\partial \rho}{\partial \mu} \, dt \leqslant 0. \qquad (5.62)$$

Finally, notice that we can write

$$\int_0^T U \frac{\partial^2 \rho}{\partial \mu^2} \, dt = \frac{\partial^2 E(U)}{\partial \mu^2} . \tag{5.63}$$

But it is clear that

$$\frac{\partial^2 U}{\partial t^2} \gtrless 0 \Rightarrow \frac{\partial^2 E(U)}{\partial \mu^2} \gtrless 0. \tag{5.64}$$

So if, as seems reasonable, it is assumed that, in addition to (4.30)—(4.32), $U(w, t)$ is such that $\partial^2 U/\partial t^2 < 0$[24] then

$$\int_0^T U \frac{\partial^2 \rho}{\partial \mu^2} \, dt < 0. \tag{5.65}$$

Thus from (5.51) together with (5.52), (5.57), (5.59), (5.61), (5.62) and (5.65),

$$\frac{\partial^2 v}{\partial \mu^2} < 0. \tag{5.66}$$

Equations (5.58) and (5.66) indicate that the marginal value of life expectancy is positive but decreasing, so that the graph of the 'value of life expectancy' function, $v(\mu)$, will have the general form depicted in figure 5.3.

As in the single-period case, it would seem desirable to proceed by investigating on the one hand the behaviour of $v(\mu)$ for extreme values of μ (this will yield the value of *large* changes in life expectancy) and on the other hand the marginal value of life expectancy evaluated at $\mu = \bar{\mu}$ (this will yield the value of *very small* changes in life expectancy). The natural counterparts in the continuous-time case to the discrete-time extremes of safety characterised by $\rho \to 0$ and $\rho \to 1$ are $\mu \to \infty$ and $\mu \to 0$ respectively.[25] As in

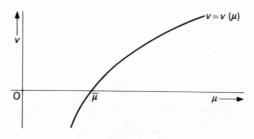

Figure 5.3.

the single-period case, a bankruptcy constraint on borrowing will place an upper bound on the amount that the individual would forfeit to effect an improvement in his own safety so that, given such a constraint on borrowing

$$\lim_{\mu \to \infty} v(\mu) \leqslant \bar{w}. \tag{5.67}$$

Similarly, if $U(w, t)$ is bounded above for each value of t (in order to avoid versions of the St Petersburg Paradox[26]) then it is possible that, for some $\mu^* > 0$,

$$\lim_{\mu \to \mu^*} v(\mu) = -\infty. \tag{5.68}$$

If (5.68) holds for some value of $\mu^* > 0$ then there exists a level of life expectancy so low that the individual is literally unwilling to accept it 'at any price' (more formally, there exists some level of life expectancy that it is impossible to induce the individual to accept however large the compensation).

Having outlined the properties of $v(\mu)$ for extreme values of μ, let us now consider the marginal value of life expectancy evaluated at $\mu = \bar{\mu}$. (Continuing the parallel with the single-period case, this would seem to be by far the most important property of $v(\mu)$ for policy purposes in view of the predominance of safety improvements having relatively small effects on individual life expectancy.) From (5.49), $\mu = \bar{\mu} \Rightarrow v = 0$, so that $(\partial v/\partial \mu)_{\bar{\mu}}$ is given simply by setting $\mu = \bar{\mu}$ and $v = 0$ in (5.50); i.e.

$$\left(\frac{\partial v}{\partial \mu} \right)_{\bar{\mu}} = \frac{ -\int_0^T \bar{U} \frac{\partial \bar{\rho}}{\partial \bar{\mu}} \, dt }{ \int_0^T \bar{\rho}(t) \bar{U}_v \, dt } \tag{5.69}$$

where $\bar{U}$ denotes $U(w, t)$ evaluated at $w = \bar{w}$ and $\bar{U}_v$ denotes U_v evaluated at $v = 0$, etc. It then follows that

$$\frac{ \partial \left(\frac{\partial v}{\partial \mu} \right)_{\bar{\mu}} }{ \partial \bar{\mu} } = \frac{ -\left(\int_0^T \bar{\rho}(t) \bar{U}_v \, dt \right) \left(\int_0^T \bar{U} \frac{\partial^2 \bar{\rho}}{\partial \bar{\mu}^2} \, dt \right) + \left(\int_0^T \bar{U} \frac{\partial \bar{\rho}}{\partial \bar{\mu}} \, dt \right) \left(\int_0^T \frac{\partial \bar{\rho}}{\partial \bar{\mu}} \bar{U}_v \, dt \right) }{ \left(\int_0^T \bar{\rho}(t) \bar{U}_v \, dt \right)^2 } \tag{5.70}$$

and

$$\frac{\partial \left(\frac{\partial v}{\partial \mu}\right)_{\bar{\mu}}}{\partial \bar{w}}$$

$$= \frac{\left(\int_0^T \bar{\rho}(t)\bar{U}_v dt\right)\left(\int_0^T \bar{U}_v \frac{\partial \bar{\rho}}{\partial \mu} dt\right) - \left(\int_0^T \bar{U} \frac{\partial \bar{\rho}}{\partial \mu} dt\right)\left(\int_0^T \bar{\rho}(t)\bar{U}_{vv} dt\right)}{\left(\int_0^T \bar{\rho}(t)\bar{U}_v dt\right)^2}.$$

(5.71)

Thus, from (5.70) in conjunction with (5.52), (5.57), (5.61) and (5.65),

$$\frac{\partial \left(\frac{\partial v}{\partial \mu}\right)_{\bar{\mu}}}{\partial \bar{\mu}} < 0$$

(5.72)

while from (5.71) in conjunction with (5.52), (5.57), (5.61) and noting that $\int_0^T \bar{\rho}(t)\bar{U}_{vv} dt < 0$,

$$\frac{\partial \left(\frac{\partial v}{\partial \mu}\right)_{\bar{\mu}}}{\partial \bar{w}} > 0.$$

(5.73)

The marginal value of life expectancy (evaluated at $\mu = \bar{\mu}$) is therefore a *decreasing* function of initial life expectancy and an *increasing* function of initial wealth. Since an increase in life expectancy can be naturally identified with an increase in safety, these results can be seen to be consistent with, but stronger than, those obtained for the marginal value of a decrease in risk in the corresponding single-period case in section 5.I.

V   THE CONTINUOUS-TIME CASE: INDIVIDUAL INSURED

Consider an individual who purchases term insurance (and/or endowment insurance and/or whole-life insurance) of the type discussed in section 4.IV. The maximum amount, v, that the individual will be prepared to forfeit to effect an improvement in safety (or the minimum sum he will accept in compensation for a deterioration in safety) will then satisfy the following condition:[27]

$$\int_0^T U(w_t - v, t)\rho(t)dt = \int_0^T U(\bar{w}_t, t)\bar{\rho}(t)dt \qquad (5.74)$$

where w_t denotes, in general, initial wealth conditional on death at time t and $\bar{w}_t$ denotes the particular value taken by w_t when the planned time-path of insurance expenditures is optimally adjusted prior to the change from $\bar{\rho}(t)$ to $\rho(t)$. Thus, if all life insurance is fair and, as in section 4.IV, w_t is written as $\bar{w} + \Delta w_t$ (so that $\bar{w}_t = \bar{w} + \Delta \bar{w}_t$), $\bar{w}$ being initial wealth prior to the purchase of life insurance, then from (4.40)

$$\int_0^T \Delta w_t \rho(t)dt = \int_0^T \Delta \bar{w}_t \bar{\rho}(t)dt = 0. \qquad (5.75)$$

By an argument similar to that developed in section 5.II, it can then be shown that expressions for $\partial v/\partial \mu$ and $\partial^2 v/\partial \mu^2$ are given by replacing $U(\bar{w} - v, t)$ by $U(w_t - v, t)$, $[\partial U(\bar{w} - v, t)]/\partial v$ by $[\partial U(w_t - v, t)]/\partial v$ etc., in equations (5.50) and (5.51). But by the argument developed in section 4.IV, at the optimal expenditure on fair life insurance of the type under discussion, $[\partial U(w_t - v, t)]/\partial v$ will be *independent* of t. It then follows, by reasoning similar to that employed in section 5.IV, that the qualitative results concerning the properties of $v(\mu)$ are *unmodified* by the purchase of (fair) life insurance.[28]

VI   THE CONTINUOUS-TIME CASE: SUMMARY

In summary, it has been shown that, whether or not an individual purchases (fair) life insurance, the value of life expectancy function, $v(\mu)$ will exhibit the following properties:

$$\frac{\partial v}{\partial \mu} > 0 \qquad (5.76)$$

and

$$\frac{\partial^2 v}{\partial \mu^2} < 0. \qquad (5.77)$$

In addition, the behaviour of $v(\mu)$ for extreme values of μ will be as shown in figure 5.4.

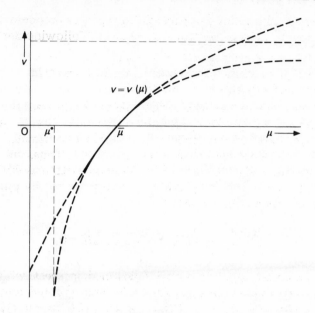

Figure 5.4.

It has also been shown that, regardless of whether or not the individual purchases life insurance, the marginal value of life expectancy, $\partial v/\partial \mu$, evaluated at the initial level of life expectancy, μ, is an unambiguously increasing function of initial wealth; i.e.

$$\frac{\partial \left(\dfrac{\partial v}{\partial \mu}\right)_{\bar{\mu}}}{\partial \bar{w}} > 0. \tag{5.78}$$

It therefore appears that life expectancy may be treated as a non-inferior good.

Finally it has been shown that, regardless of whether or not the individual purchases life insurance, the marginal value of life expectancy evaluated at $\bar{\mu}$ is a *decreasing* function of initial life expectancy; i.e.

$$\frac{\partial \left(\dfrac{\partial v}{\partial \mu}\right)_{\bar{\mu}}}{\partial \bar{\mu}} < 0. \tag{5.79}$$

The implication of (5.78) and (5.79) therefore seems to be that a conventional cost—benefit analysis will tend to direct scarce safety improvement resources towards *relatively* high-income, low-life-expectancy areas. Needless to say the distributional caveats noted in section 5.III also apply here.

It is clear, then, that when treating an increase in life expectancy as an increase in safety, the qualitative results for the continuous-time case are quite consistent with the results derived earlier for the single-period case. This is a rather encouraging conclusion, especially in view of the fact that a variation in life expectancy is the most straightforward and, indeed, the most natural formalisation of a variation in safety in a multi-period or continuous-time context.

VII   INDIRECT RISKS[29] AND NON-FATAL ACCIDENTS

Having considered the question of an individual's valuation of changes in the subjective probability of his *own* demise, it is natural to wonder whether it might be possible to investigate the individual's valuation of variations in other types of risk using a similar analytical procedure. Accordingly this section explores the means by which the earlier analysis might be modified and extended to accommodate, in particular, *indirect risks* (involving the death or injury of other people) and non-fatal accidents.

In the single-period, discrete-time case indirect risks and non-fatal accidents can be dealt with in principle simply by extending the number of mutually exclusive conditioning events for each level of initial wealth from 'life' and 'death' during the current period for the individual himself to the various mutually exclusive combinations of life, death and injury for the individual *and* those he cares about. The conditional utility functions $L(w)$ and $D(w)$ of the earlier analysis are then supplemented by as many utility functions as there are additional conditioning events. Clearly the results of an analysis extended to cover indirect risks and non-fatal accidents will depend intimately upon the properties of the various conditional utility functions and upon the signs and relative magnitudes of their first and second derivatives with respect to initial wealth. It is because of the extensive restrictions required to generate determinate results in such cases that a purely *a priori* qualitative analysis of simultaneous variations in more than one type of risk is unlikely to prove particularly fruitful.

However, provided that we are prepared to proceed on a 'piecemeal' *ceteris paribus* basis, restricting attention to variations in *just one* type of risk at a time, then it would seem possible to apply the analytical procedures developed in earlier sections to consider the value of variations in indirect risks and the risks of non-fatal accidents. Consider, for example, variations in the risk of death for individual j about whom the ith individual cares. The conditional utility functions $L(w)$ and $D(w)$ of the earlier analysis would then have to be replaced by functions $L_j(w_i)$ and $D_j(w_i)$ being the ith individual's utility functions of his *own* initial wealth w_i conditional, respectively, upon survival of and death during the current period for the jth individual. However, the qualitative restrictions on $L(w)$ and $D(w)$ specified in section IV were so weak that there appears to be no reason to believe that the same qualitative assumptions should not also apply to $L_j(w_i)$ and $D_j(w_i)$. Given that it is generally possible to purchase life insurance on the life of individuals other than oneself, then provided such insurance is taken to be effectively fair, the analysis of the value to the ith individual of changes in the risk of death to the jth individual would *precisely* parallel that developed in sections 5.I and 5.II, and the qualitative results summarised in section 5.III would apply equally to *indirect* risks of death. Similar comments would seem to apply to risks of non-fatal accident with possible reservations about the availability of opportunities for entering into fair insurance contracts.

Similarly, in a continuous-time context it would seem possible to accommodate indirect risks and non-fatal accidents by denoting the time of occurrence of the kth undesirable event by t_k and defining a utility function $U(w, t_1, t_2, \ldots t_n)$ on the set of ordered $n + 1$-tuples:

$$\{(w, t_1, t_2, \ldots t_n) | w \in R, \ 0 \leqslant t_k \leqslant T, \ k = 1 \ldots n\}$$

It would naturally be necessary in such an approach to require that if t_1 denoted the time of serious injury for any individual and t_h the time of death for the *same* individual, then

$$t_1 < t_h. \tag{5.80}$$

This suggests that the domains of U and of the generalised density function, ρ, should be restricted to accommodate such constraints, but in order to avoid technical problems with the definition of expected utility as a straightforward multiple integral it would be preferable to treat the domain of both functions as being unrestricted but to require that, for example,

$$t_1 \geqslant t_k \Rightarrow \rho(t_1, t_2, \ldots t_n) = 0. \tag{5.81}$$

Expected utility can then be written as

$$E(U) = \int_0^T \int_0^T \ldots \int_0^T U(w, t_1, t_2, \ldots t_n)$$

$$\times \rho(t_1, t_2, \ldots t_n)dt_1, dt_2, \ldots dt_n \qquad (5.82)$$

Again, it would be fruitless to attempt to specify the properties of U and ρ to the extent that would be required to allow the derivation of determinate qualitative propositions concerning the value of *simultaneous* changes in more than one type of risk. Fortunately, though, as in the single-period case, it would seem possible to apply the analysis of sections 5.IV and 5.V (with appropriate modifications) to *ceteris paribus* variations in the *indirect* risks of death. However, the same cannot be said of *ceteris paribus* variations in the direct or indirect risk of non-fatal accident. The essential reason for this is that, since it is possible that any particular individual will *never* be involved in a non-fatal accident, a counterpart to $\rho(t)$ cannot generally be assumed to exist.

VIII   EQUIVALENT VARIATIONS IN WEALTH

Up to this point the discussion has been exclusively concerned with the compensating variations in wealth associated with changes in safety. In this section we shall consider the subtly different concept of *equivalent* variations in wealth and in particular the relationship between the compensating and equivalent variations for a given change in safety.

An individual's equivalent variation in wealth for a given allocative change is defined as the amount by which the individual's wealth must be adjusted to induce him to forgo the change (if desirable) or to make him as badly off without the change as he would be with it (if undesirable). The equivalent variation is therefore the amount by which the individual's wealth must be adjusted to make him feel just as well off without the allocative change as with it. In the discussion that follows hypothetical compensation for a forgone *desirable* change is treated as a *positive* equivalent variation.

Thus for example, in the single-period, discrete-time case, given an individual who holds no life insurance, the equivalent variation, e, in wealth for a change in the subjective probability of death during the current period from $\bar{p}$ $(0 < \bar{p} < 1)$ to some other level p is given by[30]

$$(1 - p)L(\bar{w}) + pD(\bar{w}) = (1 - \bar{p})L(\bar{w} + e) + \bar{p}D(\bar{w} + e) \quad (5.83)$$

where $L(w)$, $D(w)$ and $\bar{w}$ are as defined in section 5.I.

In order to avoid excessive notational complexity, notice that setting $e = -v$,[31] we have $L(\bar{w} + e) = L(\bar{w} - v)$, $D(\bar{w} + e) = D(\bar{w} - v)$, $[\partial L(\bar{w} + e)/\partial e] = [-\partial L(\bar{w} - v)/\partial v]$ etc., so that from the definitions of L, D, L', D' etc., introduced on page 94, it follows that we can write

$$L(\bar{w} + e) = L$$
$$D(\bar{w} + e) = D$$
$$\frac{\partial L(\bar{w} + e)}{\partial e} = -L'$$
$$\frac{\partial D(\bar{w} + e)}{\partial e} = -D' \tag{5.84}$$
$$\frac{\partial^2 L(\bar{w} + e)}{\partial e^2} = L''$$
$$\frac{\partial^2 D(\bar{w} + e)}{\partial e^2} = D''.$$

Hence from (5.83) and (5.84)

$$\frac{\partial e}{\partial p} = \frac{\bar{L} - \bar{D}}{(1 - \bar{p})L' + \bar{p}D'} \tag{5.85}$$

where, as in section 5.I, $\bar{L}$ and $\bar{D}$ denote $L(w)$ and $D(w)$ respectively evaluated at $w = \bar{w}$, and

$$\frac{\partial^2 e}{\partial p^2} = \frac{(\bar{L} - \bar{D})[(1 - \bar{p})L'' + \bar{p}D''] \dfrac{\partial e}{\partial p}}{[(1 - \bar{p})L' + \bar{p}D']^2}. \tag{5.86}$$

Thus from (5.85), together with (5.7), and (5.9) and (5.11)

$$\frac{\partial e}{\partial p} < 0 \tag{5.87}$$

so that, from (5.86) together with (5.8), (5.10), (5.11) and (5.87),

$$\frac{\partial^2 e}{\partial p^2} > 0. \tag{5.88}$$

Finally notice that by setting $e = 0$ in (5.85) we obtain

$$\left(\frac{\partial e}{\partial p}\right)_{\bar{p}} = \frac{\bar{L} - \bar{D}}{(1 - \bar{p})\bar{L}' + \bar{p}\bar{D}'} \tag{5.89}$$

where, as in section 5.I, $\bar{L}'$ and $\bar{D}'$ denote L' and D' respectively evaluated at $e = 0$.

From (5.27) and (5.89) it follows that

$$\left(\frac{\partial v}{\partial p}\right)_{\bar{p}} = \left(\frac{\partial e}{\partial p}\right)_{\bar{p}}. \tag{5.90}$$

By a similar modification to the argument developed in section 5.II, the same condition can be shown to hold for the individual who *does* hold (fair) life insurance.

The result embodied in (5.90) is extremely interesting in that it indicates that the *marginal* value of a change in risk is independent of whether 'value' is defined as a compensating variation in wealth or as an equivalent variation. This markedly enhances the robustness and generality of the idea of the 'marginal value of a change in risk' earlier advocated as the single most important concept for allocative decisions implying relatively small changes in individual safety.

To summarise the results obtained so far in this section, the general form of the graph of $e(p)$ is shown in relation to that of $v(p)$ in figure 5.5.

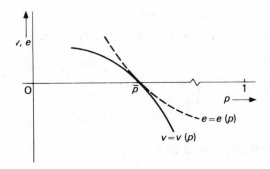

Figure 5.5.

In the continuous-time case for an individual who holds no life insurance, the equivalent variation, e, for a change in the subjective density function for time of death from $\bar{p}(t)$ to $p(t)$ is given by

$$\int_0^T U(\bar{w}, t)p(t)dt = \int_0^T U(w + e, t)\bar{p}(t)dt \tag{5.91}$$

where T and the function $U(w, t)$ are as defined in section 5.IV.

It can then be shown that, setting $e = -v$ and employing the definitions of U, U_v, U_{vv} and U_{vt} given in section 5.IV, $\partial e/\partial \mu$ and $\partial^2 e/\partial \mu^2$ are given by

$$\frac{\partial e}{\partial \mu} = \frac{-\int_0^T \bar{U} \frac{\partial \rho}{\partial \mu} dt}{\int_0^T \bar{\rho}(t) U_v dt} \qquad (5.92)$$

and

$$\frac{\partial^2 e}{\partial \mu^2} = \frac{-\int_0^T U_v \bar{\rho}(t) dt \int_0^T \bar{U} \frac{\partial^2 \rho}{\partial \mu^2} dt - \int_0^T \bar{U} \frac{\partial \rho}{\partial \mu} dt \int_0^T \bar{\rho}(t) U_{vv} \frac{\partial e}{\partial \mu} dt}{\left[\int_0^T \bar{\rho}(t) U_v dt \right]^2}$$

$$(5.93)$$

where $\bar{U}$ denotes U evaluated at $e = 0$.

From (5.92) in conjunction with (5.52) and (5.57) if follows that

$$\frac{\partial e}{\partial \mu} > 0. \qquad (5.94)$$

Also setting $\rho(t) = \bar{\rho}(t)$ and $e = 0$ in (5.92) we obtain

$$\left(\frac{\partial e}{\partial \mu} \right)_{\bar{\mu}} = \frac{-\int_0^T \bar{U} \frac{\partial \bar{\rho}}{\partial \mu} dt}{\int_0^T \bar{\rho}(t) \bar{U}_v dt} \qquad (5.95)$$

so that from (5.69) and (5.95)

$$\left(\frac{\partial v}{\partial \mu} \right)_{\bar{\mu}} = \left(\frac{\partial e}{\partial \mu} \right)_{\bar{\mu}}. \qquad (5.96)$$

It is, however, impossible to infer the sign of $\partial^2 e/\partial \mu^2$ from (5.93) and the various results established in section 5.IV (this is because the first term in the numerator of (5.93) is *negative* while the second term is *positive*).

Identical qualitative results can be shown to hold for the individual who does buy life insurance.

Thus, with the exception of the indeterminacy concerning $\partial^2 e/\partial \mu^2$, the continuous-time results again constitute a natural extension of the single-period results. In particular, (5.96) indicates that the marginal value of life expectancy evaluated at $\mu = \bar{\mu}$ is independent of whether 'value' is construed as a compensating variation or, alternatively, as an equivalent variation. Again, this would seem to enhance considerably the robustness and generality of the notion.

IX   THE 'MARGINAL VALUE OF A CHANGE IN RISK' AND THE 'VALUE OF SAVING A LIFE'

In the single-period analysis it was argued that the concept of the 'marginal value of a change in risk' is of primary importance for cost—benefit analysis in the health and safety fields. This is because in the majority of safety-improvement programmes it is not known whose lives are going to be saved; so that, if the programme is expected to save s unspecified lives during the current period in a population of N people (where s is very much smaller than N), then for each individual member of society the change in safety represents an essentially *marginal* change in individual risk.

However from the social decision-maker's point of view it is natural to regard the anticipated saving of s lives as generating a benefit worth $s \times$ 'the (average) value per life saved', V, the latter presumably comprising at least three components:

(a) the (average) value of avoided real resource costs per life saved (V_1);
(b) the (average) value of avoided loss of net output per life saved (V_2);
(c) the (average) value of a human life *per se* (V_3).

This component is due to society's aversion to the event of death *per se* whereas V_1 and V_2 are a result of society's aversion to the economic losses occasioned by death.

The total benefit, B, generated by the safety improvement would then be given by

$$B = sV = s(V_1 + V_2 + V_3). \qquad (5.97)$$

The question that now arises is how the essentially non-marginal concept, V_3, is related to the marginal value of a change in risk. It would certainly seem at first sight that the two ideas are fundamentally different and that a strictly 'potential Pareto-improvement' view of cost—benefit analysis requires the rejection of the V_3 approach in favour of the explicitly marginal idea. Indeed, this was the position advocated in section 2.XIII in the critique of the work of Reynolds, Dawson and Abraham and Thedié, each of whom approached the problem in terms of a value per life saved, V, comprising, broadly speaking, the three components V_1, V_2 and V_3 defined above. *However it turns out that* V_3 *and the marginal value of a change in risk can be very simply related provided that* V_3 *is given a strictly 'potential Pareto-improvement' interpretation.*

Suppose for the sake of simplicity that individuals are concerned only for their own safety. A safety improvement that affords the ith individual a small change δp_i in the subjective probability of his own death during the current period, $(i = 1 \ldots N)$, then implies an *aggregate*-compensating variation, C, for the change in safety *per se* satisfying

$$C = \sum_{i=1}^{N} \left(\frac{\partial v_i}{\partial p_i} \right)_{\bar{p}_i} \cdot \delta p_i. \tag{5.98}$$

Now consider the safety improvement that is expected to save s lives during the current period in a population of N people. In the absence of any further information it would seem most reasonable to assume that, from the point of view of each individual member of the population, the safety improvement affords a reduction of s/N in the subjective probability of death during the current period so that we can write

$$\delta p_i = -\frac{s}{N} \ (i = 1 \ldots N). \tag{5.99}$$

From (5.98) and (5.99) it then follows that, provided s is very small in relation to N, we may write

$$C = \frac{s \left[\sum_{i=1}^{N} -\left(\frac{\partial v_i}{\partial p_i} \right)_{\bar{p}_i} \right]}{N}. \tag{5.100}$$

But on a strict 'potential Pareto-improvement' interpretation of V_3 it would be necessary to regard V_3 as *defined* by

$$C \equiv sV_3 \tag{5.101}$$

so that, from (5.100) and (5.101)

$$V_3 = \frac{\sum_{i=1}^{N} -\left(\frac{\partial v_i}{\partial p_i} \right)_{\bar{p}_i}}{N}. \tag{5.102}$$

That is, V_3 *is simply the average (over the relevant population) of the 'marginal value of a decrease in risk', the latter being precisely as defined in section 5.I.*

If we wish to recognise the fact that most people will value a change in risk for other people — especially those they care about — then by a similar argument V_3 would be given by[32]

$$V_3 = \frac{\sum\limits_{i=1}^{N} \sum\limits_{j=1}^{N} -\left(\frac{\partial v_i}{\partial p_j}\right)_{\bar{p}_j}}{N} \tag{5.103}$$

where $-(\partial v_i/\partial p_j)_{p_j}$ is the marginal value to the ith individual of a decrease in risk for the jth individual.[33]

Again, V_3 may be regarded as the average 'marginal value of a decrease in risk' but in this case the latter must be construed to include, for each individual, the marginal value of decreases in *all* relevant risks both direct *and* indirect (in Mishan's sense).

It is clear, then, that, given the appropriate definition of V_3, it is possible to express the 'value per life saved', V, in terms of the relatively uncontentious 'savings in real resource costs', V_1, and 'losses of net output', V_2, together with a population average of the 'marginal value of a decrease in risk'. In this way the apparently irreconcilable disparities of the concepts of a 'value per life saved' and the 'marginal value of a decrease in risk' are completely eliminated and the two ideas shown to have a common base. In view of this, the results of section 5.VIII concerning the relationship between equivalent and compensating variations (and in particular the invariance of the marginal value of a change in risk with respect to whether 'value' is treated as a compensating or as an equivalent variation) acquire special significance. Furthermore, the qualitative results summarised in section 5.III (concerning the impact of changes in initial risk and initial wealth on the marginal value of a decrease in risk) can be seen to have immediate relevance for the 'value per life saved'.

X   FROM QUALITATIVE TO QUANTITATIVE RESULTS

Since qualitative analysis of the value of changes in safety has yielded an encouragingly wide variety of results and insights, it is natural to wish to attempt to obtain *quantitative* information by estimating the appropriate parameters and functions from the analysis developed in this chapter.

There are generally two broad avenues of approach to such an estimation exercise. *Either* one may eschew all data sources *except* the market place, relying entirely upon the revelation of private preferences through choices among alternatives presented through a market mechanism, *or* one may utilise direct inquiry and experimental methods in an attempt to obtain a richer variety of data than is available through observation of market choices alone. However, it was argued earlier that the 'public goods' nature of most safety improvements severely restricts the range of safety-improvement devices that are supplied through markets, and it was essentially because of this paucity of market-generated data that the problem of the value of safety was approached in a largely *a priori* manner from very general (and, one hopes, plausible) assumptions concerning individual choice under uncertainty. For similar reasons one would not be optimistic about gleaning a sufficiently rich body of data concerning market choices involving the types of risk under discussion to permit estimation of, say, the 'marginal value of a change in risk' for a sample of individuals.[34] The only alternative is therefore an experimental, direct-inquiry approach. The next chapter outlines an example of such an approach.

APPENDIX: MORTALITY TABLES AND THE DENSITY FUNCTION, $\rho(t)$

Mortality statistics are typically presented in the following format: for each (relevant) positive integer value of x, mortality tables give the number, $l(x)$, of individuals of age x surviving from an initial population,[35] $l(x_0)$, of individuals all of age x_0. The purpose of this appendix is to outline the relationship between the function $l(x)$ — suitably generalised to accommodate non-integer values of x — and the *objective* counterpart to the subjective probability density function, $\rho(t)$. (This objective version of $\rho(t)$ is the one that would be relevant for an individual who takes an essentially 'relative frequency' view of his own chance of survival to various ages and ignores additional factors such as personal medical history.)

Consider an individual of age a. It will be recalled that $\rho(t)$ was defined as the subjective probability density for death at age $a + t$. The objective counterpart to $\rho(t)$ is therefore the probability density function for death at age $a + t$ *conditional* upon survival to age a, which will be denoted $\rho(t/a)$. This conditional density function will then be related to $l(x)$ as follows:

$$\int_{t_1}^{t_2} \rho(t/a)dt = \frac{l(a + t_1) - l(a + t_2)}{l(a)} \qquad (5.104)$$

so that, if $l(x)$ is treated as continuous and differentiable,[36] it follows from (5.104) that

$$\rho(t/a) = -\frac{1}{l(a)} \frac{dl}{dx}\bigg|_{x = a + t}, \qquad (t \geqslant a) \qquad (5.105)$$

Now according to '*A 1949–52*' *Tables for Assured Lives*, Vol. 1, the general form of the graph of $l(x)$ is as shown in figure 5.6.

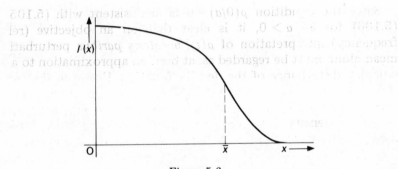

Figure 5.6.

It is clear, then, that

$$l'(x) < 0, \qquad (x > 0) \qquad (5.106)$$

and

$$l''(x) < 0, \qquad (0 \leqslant x < \bar{x})$$
$$l''(x) = 0, \qquad (x = \bar{x}) \qquad (5.107)$$
$$l''(x) > 0, \qquad (x > \bar{x})$$
$$\bar{x} \simeq 75$$

Thus if $a < \bar{x}$ then the graph of $\rho(t/a)$ will have the general form depicted in figure 5.7, while if $a > \bar{x}$ then the graph of $\rho(t/a)$ will be of the form shown in figure 5.8. Clearly in *neither* case is it possible

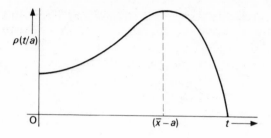

Figure 5.7.

to perturb $\rho(t/a)$ by a *strictly ceteris paribus* variation in mean: the only circumstances under which this *would* be possible being $\rho(0/a) = 0$ so that a *ceteris paribus* increase in mean could be effected by a simple change of origin (i.e. by a rightward shift in the graph of $\rho(t/a)$) as shown in figure 5.9.

Since the condition $\rho(0/a) = 0$ is inconsistent with (5.105) and (5.106) for all $a > 0$, it is clear that on an objective (relative-frequency) interpretation of $\rho(t)$, a *ceteris paribus* perturbation in mean alone must be regarded as, at best, an approximation to a more complex disturbance of the density function. However, the fact that the *objective* density function $\rho(t/a)$ cannot generally take the form shown in figure 5.9 does *not* rule out the possibility that the *subjective* density function $\rho(t)$ — influenced by a wide variety of factors besides mortality statistics — might do so. It should be noted, though, that a strict *ceteris paribus* increase in the mean of $\rho(t)$ would then imply that the individual viewed his death during the interval $0 \leqslant t \leqslant \tau$ as an impossibility. Such a situation seems unlikely, to say the least.

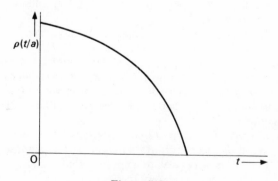

Figure 5.8.

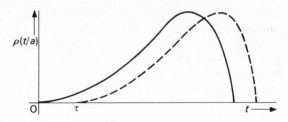

Figure 5.9.

For these reasons it seems best to regard the analysis of sections 5.IV—5.VI as applying to those cases in which the perturbation in the mean of $\rho(t)$ is large in relation to the perturbation in other moments.

NOTES

1. This chapter is essentially a development of ideas originally discussed in Jones-Lee (1969, 1974). In certain respects the basic postulates of the analysis are similar to those adopted in Usher (1973) — see section 2.IX. For example, both analyses employ the expected utility-maximisation hypothesis and both place heavy emphasis upon the value of small changes in risk. However, there are many very important ways in which the analyses differ. In particular, we recognise the possibility of purchasing life insurance and allow the individual to show concern for other people. We also employ a set of assumptions concerning the properties of utility functions, which, although less specific and restrictive than Usher's, none the less preclude the pathological possibilities noted in section 2.IX. In view of these and many other differences, the analysis developed in the present chapter is, hopefully, rather more general than Usher's and in addition deals with a wider range of problems.
2. See section 1.I for a discussion of compensating variations.
3. See for example, Reynolds (1956) and Dawson (1967).
4. It would seem especially important that we should do this in view of the controversy associated with the question of whether allocative decisions should be based upon compensating or equivalent variations. For opposing views see Mishan (1972) pp. 130 and Foster and Neuburger (1974). See also n. 12 of chapter 1.
5. Provided that bankruptcy imposes no limitation on borrowing, it is possible for v to exceed $\bar{w}$. However, if bankruptcy *does* impose a borrowing limitation, then it is necessary to impose the restriction, $v \leqslant \bar{w}$. Strictly speaking it would then be necessary to write (5.4) as a weak inequality with

a complementary-slackness condition for the restriction on v. For simplicity, the possibility of bankruptcy will be ignored in what follows though it will be necessary to give it explicit consideration when dealing with the value of complete elimination of the risk of death.

6. v will therefore be *negative* for $p > \bar{p}$.

7. Notice that (5.13) and (5.14) *exclude* the case in which $p = 1$. This is because, if $D' = 0$ (a possibility that is quite consistent with (5.9)), then $\partial v / \partial p$ and $\partial^2 v / \partial p^2$ would, from (5.5) and (5.6), be undefined when $p = 1$.

8. Notice that $\partial v / \partial p$ is the marginal value of an *increase* in risk and is therefore negative. By contrast $-(\partial v / \partial p)$ is the marginal value of a *decrease* in risk and is consequently positive.

9. It is assumed throughout that this function is defined for all values of U that are considered. Thus, it is assumed that if $L(w)$ is bounded below then the greatest lower bound, α, is such that $U > \alpha$ for all values of U considered, while if $L(w)$ is bounded above, the least upper bound α is assumed to be such that $U < \alpha$ for all values of U considered.

10. Even if it were possible to do so, and it is *not* being suggested for one moment that it is, in fact, possible.

11. See n. 5, above.

12. From (5.11) it then follows that $\alpha \geqslant \beta$.

13. Notice that if (5.24) holds then for $dL/dw > 0$ it must be the case that $\alpha > \beta$ so that p^* is well-defined.

14. $v(p)$ is then defined only in the interval $0 \leqslant p < p^*$.

15. However, the same remarks apply to the possibility of a bankruptcy constraint as those outlined in n. 5 above.

16. Throughout this section the term 'optimal insurance premium' is intended to refer to the insurance premium that satisfies the optimality conditions established in the preceding chapter. (It can be shown that the insurance premium, x, which maximises v subject to (5.32) will always satisfy such conditions.)

17. In fact this requires that we assume that a change in p causes changes in x (and hence z) which are of second-order of smallness compared with the change in v — this assumption is implicit throughout the current section. This seems to be a not unreasonable assumption, certainly for small changes in p.

    If the changes in x and z are not ignored then, strictly speaking, the derivative $\partial v / \partial p$ is — as pointed out by Cook and Graham (1974) — given by

$$\frac{\partial v}{\partial p} = \frac{\Theta - \Psi}{(1-p)\Theta' + p\Psi'} - (x + z)$$

18. This condition holds, of course, only if we fully recognize the dependence of x and z on p. However there is no inconsistency with the 'second-order of smallness' argument in footnote 17 since (5.39) is a precise condition and footnote 17 is concerned with adequate approximations.

19. Notice that, in contrast to (5.13), the result given in (5.41) does not exclude the case in which $p = 1$. This is because any individual who purchases fair insurance and for whom (5.7) holds *must* have $D' \neq 0$ (see footnote 7). *However*, in view of the fact that the 'second-order of smallness' argument in footnote 17 applies only to small changes in p, the results in (5.41) and (5.42) have (strictly speaking) been demonstrated in the insured case only for values of p in some neighbourhood of $\bar{p}$.

20. See ns. 7 and 19 (especially the reservations in 19).

21. See chapter 1, especially section 1.I.

22. As usual, we ignore the possibility of a binding bankruptcy constraint. Notice also that, because of the absence of life insurance, initial wealth is treated as parametric in this section (see n. 10, chapter 4).

23. For a discussion of this point, see the appendix to the current chapter.

24. This condition appears to follow immediately if one assumes that individuals are *physically* as well as *financially* risk-averse.

25. For example, one would naturally identify an increase in safety with a *decrease* in the probability, p, of death in the current period and an *increase* in life expectancy, μ.

26. See chapter 4, n. 6.

27. Again, we ignore the possibility of a binding bankruptcy constraint.

28. Notice however that these results are based upon a similar 'second-order of smallness' assumption (concerning changes in premia and sums assured) to that adopted in section (5.3) (see ns. 17—19). Notice also the contrast with the single period case in which the 'insured' and uninsured' results were similar but not *identical*.

29. In Mishan's sense of the term (see section 2.VII).

30. Ignoring, as usual, the possibility of a binding bankruptcy constraint.

31. Notice that this is purely and simply a definitional convenience. It is not intended as the assertion that the value of v satisfying equation (5.4) for particular values of p and $\bar{p}$ will be thus related to the value of e satisfying (5.83) for the same probabilities.

32. Assuming that (5.99) holds not only for each individual's degrees of belief about his own death but also for each individual's degree of belief about each other individual's death.

33. Needleman is currently engaged in research designed to elicit versions of this marginal value for close relatives from data concerning willingness to act as donor in kidney transplants.

34. It should be noted, however, that recent attempts to estimate the value of life from wage premia for risky occupations (see section 2.X above, especially n. 34) represent a potentially fruitful first step in this direction (although one suspects that those who voluntarily participate in risky occupations will yield a very biased sample of attitudes to safety).

35. Known as the 'radix' of the mortality tables.

36. By definition, $l(x)$ should strictly speaking take on only *integer* values. However it is analytically most convenient, and seems only a slight abstraction from reality, to assume that $l(x)$ is a continuous (and differentiable) function.

REFERENCES

Cook, P. J. and Graham, D. A. 'The Demand for Insurance and Protection: The Case of Irreplaceable Commodities' Mimeo (1974)

Dawson, R. F. F. *Cost of Road Accidents in Great Britain* London, Road Research Laboratory Ministry of Transport (1967)

Foster, C. D. and Neuburger, H. L. I. 'The Ambiguity of the Consumer's Surplus Measure of Welfare Change' *Oxford Economic Papers* (1974)

Jones-Lee, M. W. 'Valuation of Reduction in Probability of Death by Road Accident' *Journal of Transport Economics and Policy* (January 1969)

Jones-Lee, M. W. 'The Value of Changes in the Probability of Death or Injury' *Journal of Political Economy* (July/August 1974)

Mishan, E. J. *Cost—Benefit Analysis* London, Allen and Unwin (1972)

Reynolds, D. J. 'The Cost of Road Accidents' *Journal of the Royal Statistical Society* (1956)

Usher, D. 'An Imputation to the Measure of Economic Growth for Changes in Life Expectancy' in *NBER Conference on Research in Income and Wealth* (1971)

6. The Value of Changes in Safety and Longevity: An Estimation Procedure

> *In the circumstances, economists seriously concerned with coming to grips with the magnitudes may have to brave the disdain of their colleagues and consider the possibility that data yielded by surveys based on the questionnaire method are better than none . . .* Mishan 'Evaluation of Life and Limb: A Theoretical Approach'

The purpose of this chapter is to outline an experimental procedure capable of generating sufficient data to permit estimation of the functions $v(p)$ and $v(\mu)$ and in particular the 'marginal value of a change in risk' appropriately defined for each of $v(p)$ and $v(\mu)$. It must be stressed that what follows is *not* intended as a comprehensive and definitive exercise in the empirical estimation of the value of safety, but rather as an indication of a *possible* method of obtaining quantitative estimates together with examples of the application of this method. The reasons for employing experimental methods (rather than direct observations of market transactions and behaviour) have already been discussed in earlier chapters and will not be reiterated here. However, it would be valuable to begin with a general discussion of the role and scientific status of experimental procedures of the type advocated in this chapter.

I EXPERIMENTAL RESULTS: FACT OR FICTION?

There are basically two types of so-called 'experimental' approach to the generation of data concerning choice in economics. In the first type of procedure (which we shall call the 'laboratory' approach) the subject is invited to make a choice from a set of alternatives under artificial (i.e. laboratory rather than market) conditions and the selected alternative is noted. In the second type of procedure (referred to as the 'direct inquiry' approach) one simply asks the subject to *imagine* which element he would select from a hypothetical set of alternatives, and to report his imagined selection.

The laboratory approach has two significant shortcomings. In the first place it is often simply not feasible to construct a 'real' laboratory instance of many types of decision problem in which one might be interested. For example, suppose one wished to estimate the form of the function $L(w)$ of section 5.I for a wide range of values of w. The laboratory approach would then require that the subject be offered a series of gambles,[1] including some with very large payoffs. It is patently not feasible for most researchers to do this. The second objection to the laboratory approach is that there is no guarantee that an individual who would make a given choice from a particular range of alternatives under real (e.g. market) conditions will make the same choice from an identical set of alternatives under *laboratory* conditions. The very fact that the individual is aware that he is in a laboratory situation may influence his choice.

The first of these objections to the laboratory approach is clearly directed at its feasibility rather than its fundamental scientific status. Moreover, most scientists would probably consider the second objection in the context of the problem of *controlling* the various determinants of choice, the basic method being viewed as a more-or-less respectable exercise from a scientific point of view.

The status of the direct inquiry approach is altogether far more controversial. While the first objection to the laboratory approach clearly does not apply (the subject can be asked to '*imagine*' his response to *any* situation whatever), many scientists and philosophers of science hold that introspection is *not* a legitimate source of the kind of empirical material with which science should (in their opinion) be concerned. Instead, advocates of this view hold that, in order to qualify as the proper subject matter of science, empirical propositions must (in principle) be capable of verification by anyone sufficiently interested. Typical of such a 'universally[2] testable' proposition is the scientific 'law' that asserts that, whenever an event of type A occurs, then so too does an event of type α. Clearly it is open to anyone who wishes to do so to test such a proposition and, if it is false, to disconfirm it. However, since only the *subject himself* can introspect about his own preferences and imagined choices, it is clear why those who subscribe to the view outlined above would not allow the reported results of introspection to form the basis of a scientific discussion.

However this position does seem rather extreme. While the possibility of universal verification is clearly *desirable*, the view that it is *essential* appears to derive from nothing more substantial than rigid adherence to a rather arbitrary specification of what constitutes the legitimate source of empirical material. It seems nihilistic in the extreme to preclude introspection as a potential source of data *ab initio*, especially if it seems likely that no other satisfactory data sources are available. Of course, one would presumably wish to establish criteria by which the veracity of the reported results of introspection might be judged. In this respect there seem to be two primary reasons why the reported results might not be true indications of how the subject would actually behave in a real-choice situation. First of all there are probably particular kinds of choice that may be difficult, if not impossible, to imagine (e.g., the layman might find difficulty with military decisions in which improved chances of mission success must be weighed against increased equipment loss and casualty rates). Secondly, there are clearly circumstances in which the subject would have a strong incentive to misrepresent his preferences and imagined choice (e.g., the classic case of the individual who understates his preferences for the level of provision of a public good in the belief that this will reduce the contribution that he will be required to make to its provision). However, in any particular case it should at least be possible to make an educated guess at whether either of these factors is likely to represent a serious problem. Moreover it will frequently be possible to execute some kind of 'consistency test' in which the reported results of introspection are compared with observed behaviour. However, the feasibility of either of these screening devices obviously depends to a large extent upon the precise nature of the experiment under consideration, so that in order to assess the potential effectiveness of the particular experimental method to be employed in this chapter it will be necessary to consider in some detail the key features of the experiment.

II   THE EXPERIMENT

The object of the experiment is to generate data concerning $v(p)$ and $v(\mu)$ in the neighbourhood of $\bar{p}$ and $\bar{\mu}$ respectively. This was done by confronting the subject with a series of choices between hypothetical alternatives differing only in (a) the level of p (or μ) and (b) the level of wealth for the individual. More precisely, in the case of $v(p)$, the subject was asked what premium or discount on a standard air fare would just induce him to accept particular variations in airline safety records. In order to generate data concerning $v(\mu)$ a similar procedure was employed with aircraft accident rates replaced by variations in life expectancy and air fares replaced by non-recoverable premia or discounts on house purchase prices.

The entire exercise was conducted by questionnaire, individuals being invited to complete this at their leisure and return it anonymously. The actual questionnaire is reproduced below.

'VALUE OF SAFETY' QUESTIONNAIRE

1. Suppose that for various reasons you have decided to make a particular journey by air and have the choice of travelling on one of two airlines, A or B. These two airlines use the same type of aircraft and provide effectively identical services (same journey time, same route, same frequency of flights, similar food and in-flight facilities etc.)

   Airline A's fare is £100. Furthermore, airline A has a recent safety record of 2 fatal crashes in 500,000 flights.

   At what fare would you *just* be induced to fly by airline B rather than airline A if the recent safety record for airline B is:

   (a) 0 fatal crashes in 500,000 flights   _____

   (b) 1 „   „   „   „   „   _____

   (c) 5 „   „   „   „   „   _____

   (d) 10 „   „   „   „   „   _____

   (e) 20 „   „   „   „   „   _____

   If in any instance you would not fly by airline B at any price then put 'X'.

   Assume that you are to be paid fixed expenses of £100 for the journey and that you will be unaccompanied by wife or other members of your family You should also assume that the recent crash record is the *only* available information concerning the safety of each airline.

2. Assuming that you would again be paid expenses of £100/journey, would your answers to question 1 be different if the journey was to be made once per week for one year? If the answer is 'yes', then indicate the modified fares in parentheses beside the answers to question 1. If the answer is 'no', then write 'no' here.

3. Suppose that you face a job location decision, the alternatives being areas A and B. (Assume that the option of remaining in your current location is not available.) Suppose further that considering all pros and cons *except* (a) house prices and (b) the impact of environmental pollution on life expectancy* you are indifferent between the two alternative locations.

If area A has a 'normal' level of environmental pollution (so that your life expectancy will be as given by standard mortality tables), indicate the premium or discount on area B house prices relative to area A which would *just* induce you to choose area B if the environmental pollution for area B is such as to change your life expectancy by:

(a) adding 1 year   _____ / _____

(b) adding 5 years   _____ / _____

(c) adding 10 years   _____ / _____

(d) subtracting 1 year   _____ / _____

(e) subtracting 5 years   _____ / _____

(f) subtracting 10 years   _____ / _____

Give one set of answers for the case in which the effect on life expectancy applies only to yourself and (if you have a family) one set for the case in which it applies both to yourself and your family. *Give premia and discounts in absolute amounts of money rather than as percentages.* Assume that you plan to remain in the new location for a sufficiently long time for any differential capital gains on house resale to be negligible (i.e. the premium or discount on current purchase price is to be an effective once-for-all lump sum gain or loss).

*   An increase in life expectancy is an increase in the statistical mean age at death and will therefore inevitably affect the *entire* probability density function for time of death. In this case you may assume that there is negligible error in treating this as an effective rightward shift in the density function, i.e.

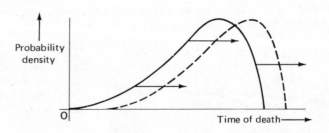

4. What is your current age?

5. What is your current salary?

6. What is your current occupation?

How does such a procedure fare by the criteria outlined in section 6.I (i.e., is there strong evidence to suggest that the subject would (a) find difficulty in imagining his response to such choices and/or (b) have any incentive to misrepresent his imagined response)? As far as deliberate misrepresentation is concerned, there is no apparent reason why a subject should wish to distort his answers to questions of the sort outlined above unless, of course, he appreciates that the ultimate object of the exercise is to elicit his preferences over levels of provision of what is essentially a public good. Even so, it is rather unlikely that the majority of subjects would possess sufficient technical expertise to distort their answers in such a way as to ensure a consistent implicit understatement of the 'true' preferences for safety improvement. However there is greater cause for concern about the capacity of most subjects for *imagining* their response to this type of question in the first place.

The whole exercise involves the subject in introspection about choices between alternatives where the choice affects the probability of his own death. Can the average subject be expected to do this? While the initial response to this question is typically pessimistic, it is worth recalling that most individuals make this sort of choice daily, if not several times each day: practically every locational or occupational decision implicitly affects an individual's safety and it does not seem unreasonable to assume that most people are aware of this in at least a proportion of cases (who can seriously claim to be ignorant of the potential consequences of a decision not to wear car seat-belts?). Thus, in view of the fact that most people have had extensive practice in taking such decisions, there is probably less cause for scepticism about the proposed experimental procedure than initially appears to be the case. It would therefore seem rather unreasonable to discount the experiment either on the grounds of the potential untruthfulness of subjects or the inherent difficulty of introspecting about the broad category of choices involved.

There remains, however, a serious problem associated with the estimation of subjective probabilities. While individuals may be well versed in taking decisions involving effects on their own safety, they are probably not accustomed to doing so in terms of explicit evaluation of the probability of survival.[3] In view of this it is important to elicit subjective probabilities *indirectly* by characterising alternatives in terms of some simple chance mechanism such as the airline accident rates. In this way the subject may, if he wishes, completely avoid the use of probability concepts though it is of course necessary for the experimenter to

(a) assume that the subject's degrees of belief can be legitimately formalised as subjective probabilities; and then
(b) estimate these subjective probabilities from the characteristics of the hypothetical chance mechanism.

In a sense, then, one's confidence in the experimental results will depend upon one's belief in the legitimacy of (a) and the feasibility of (b).

III   RESULTS

For illustrative purposes the experiment was conducted (early in 1975) for a small sample of individuals. Of some 90 people who were sent the questionnaire, about 30 responded. Since this sample consisted mainly of academics and research workers, together with a few public-sector employees, it could hardly be regarded as a cross-section of the population.[4] None the less, despite the heavy bias towards a few specialised occupations, there is considerable variation in age and salary within the sample.

The questionnaire responses (other than biographical details) are shown in the first 11 columns of table 6.1.[5] For each questionnaire, answers to question 1 are entered as the *upper* row of figures in colums (1a)—(1e), while answers to question 2 are entered as the *lower* row of figures in columns (1a)—(1e). Similarly, answers to the first part of question 3 are entered as the upper row of figures in columns (3a)—(3f), while answers to the second part of question 3 are entered as the lower row of figures in colums (3a)—(3f). Estimates of $-(\partial v/\partial p)_{\bar{p}}$ and $(\partial v/\partial \mu)_{\bar{\mu}}$ are given in the last two columns of table 6.1. For each questionnaire, the upper figure for $-(\partial v/\partial p)_{\bar{p}}$ is an estimate based on the safety variation for a single journey, while the lower figure is an estimate based on the safety variation effective on a weekly journey over a period of one year. The upper figure for $(\partial v/\partial \mu)_{\bar{\mu}}$ is an estimate of the marginal value of changes in longevity applicable only to the subject, while the lower figure is an estimate of the marginal value of changes in longevity applicable to the subject *and* his family. These estimates were obtained on the basis of the following argument.

Table 6.1.* Summary of Responses to 'Value of Safety' Questionnaire

Question No.	(1a)	(1b)	(1c)	(1d)	(1e)	(3a)	(3b)	(3c)	(3d)	(3e)	(3f)	Age	Salary	Occupation†	$-\left(\dfrac{\partial v}{\partial p}\right)_{\bar p}$	$\left(\dfrac{\partial v}{\partial \mu}\right)_{\bar\mu}$
1	200	125	50	X	X	0	1000	4000	−3000	−5000	X	30	3500	A	12.5m	1500
	150	110	X	X	X	2000	5000	10000	−8000	−10000	X				5.0m	5000
2	110	105	85	75	60	100	200	400	−100	−1500	−6000	32	5500	A	2.5m	100
	110	105	85	75	60	100	200	400	−100	−1500	−6000				2.5m	100
3	100	100	X	X	X	0	1000	2000	0	−3000	X	27	3100	A		150
	100	100	X	X	X	0	1000									
4	100	100	100—	X	X	0	2500	2500	0	−2500	−5000	26	2000	R		400
	100	100	X	X	X											
5	110	105	X	X	X	500	800	1000	0	−1500	−2500	45	6000	A	2.5m	250
	110	105	X	X	X	500	800	1000	0	−1500	−2500				2.5m	250
6	110	105	75	0	X	1500	6000	10000	−5000	X	X	40	8200	A	4.2m	3250
	115	110	50	X	X										8.3m	
7	100	100	90	70	50	250	2000	3500	−1000	−8000	−9000	23	2200	R	1.7m	625
	100	100	85	60	30	250	3000	5000	−1000	−9000	X				2.5m	625
8	100.37	100.19	99.39	98.78	97.57	200	900	1600	−300	−1800	−5000	30	3000	R	0.08m	250
	100.37	100.19	99.39	98.78	97.57	300	1350	2400	−450	−2700	−7500				0.08m	375
9	100	100	100	X	X	500	1500	3000	−500	−8000	−20000	28	3000	A		500
	100	100	100	X	X	1000	3000	5000	−700	−10000	−40000					850
10	130	120	80	50	20	1000	1500	2000	−500	−1500	−2500	37	4000	R	3.6m	750
	105	102	90	70	40	1200	2000	3000	−1000	−2000	−3500				1.8m	1100
11	150	105	40	X	X	1000	20000	30000	−1000	X	X	34	5000	A	2.5m	1000
	120	102	X	X	X	5000	25000	30000	−5000	X	X				1.0m	5000

(Continued)

Table 6.1.* Summary of Responses to 'Value of Safety' Questionnaire (Continued)

Question No.	(1a)	(1b)	(1c)	(1d)	(1e)	(3a)	(3b)	(3c)	(3d)	(3e)	(3f)	Age	Salary	Occupation†	$-\left(\dfrac{\partial v}{\partial p}\right)\big/\bar{p}$	$\left(\dfrac{\partial v}{\partial \mu}\right)\big/\bar{\mu}$
12	105 105	101 101	98 95	95 90	90 80	0	300	1000	0	−800	−1500	25	2200	R	0.5m 0.5m	150
13	150 125	125 110	X X	X X	X X	1000 2000	3000 5000	5000 10000	−2000 X	X X	X X	49	5500	A	12.5m 5.0m	1500 2000
14	90 90	90 90	90 75	X X	X X	−1000 −1000	2500 2500	5000 5000	−1000 −1000	−5000 −5000	X X	31	3400	A		
15	102 101.5	101 101	90 20	10 X	X X	1000	3000	5000	−5000	X	X	25	2700	A	0.5m 0.5m	3000
16	105 105	102 102	90 70	50 10	5 X	100 300	1000 1500	1000 1500	−1000 −2000	−7500 X	X X	34	4500	A	1.0m 1.0m	550 1150
17	70 60	98 95	80 70	70 60	60 50	500	800	1500	−500	−2000	−4000	25	2300	A		500
18	100 100	100 100	X X	X X	X X	0	2000	2000	0	−3000	−5000	36	4000	A		330
19	105 100	100 100	X X	X X	X X	0 0	5000 5000	5000 5000	0 0	X X	X X	53	6800	A	2.5m	830 830
20	100 100	100 100	100 100	50 50	X X	0 0	0 0	500 500	0 0	−5000 −5000	−10000 −10000	50	6000	A	2.5m 2.5m	45 45
21	105 110	100 105	90 75	60 X	X X	50	350	1000	−200	−1750	X	23	2200	R	2.5m 2.5m	125
22	100 100	100 100	100 100	100 100	100 100	0 0	0 0	X X	0 0	0 0	X X	26	2300	R		
23	100 100	100 100	95 98	90 X	90 X	0 0	1000 1000	2000 2000	−1000 −1000	−5000 −5000	−8000 −8000	28	2900	A	1.0m 0.3m	500 500

24	100 / 100	100 / 100	85 / 85	X / X	X / X	500 / 500	1500 / 2000	2500 / 4000	−1000 / −2000	−4000 / X	X / X	49	7000	A	2.5m / 2.5m	750
25	100 / 100	100 / 100	100 / 100	90 / 90	70 / 70	0 / 0	500 / 500	1000 / 1000	0 / 0	X / X	X / X	32	3700	A	1.0m / 1.0m	83 / 83
26	105 / 100.5	101 / 100.1	90 / 95	X / X	X / X	200	2000	5000	−200	−6000	X	26	2600	R	0.5m / 0.05m	200
27	105 / 105	100 / 100	X / X	X / X	X / X	0	200	800	0	−1000	−3000	24	2500	R	2.5m / 2.5m	33
28	100 / 100	100 / 100	50 / 50	X / X	X / X	1000 / 4000	5000 / 20000	10000 / 40000	−3000 / −15000	−15000 / −75000	−30000 / −150000	47	8000	A	8.3m / 8.3m	2000 / 9500
29	110 / 110	105 / 105	95 / 95	90 / 90	80 / 80	1000	1500	2000	−1000	−1500	−2000	30	3000	A	2.5m / 2.5m	1000
30	110	108 / 105	85 / 90	82 / 85	80 / 75	5000	7000	70000	X	X	X	25	3000	A	4.0m / 2.5m	5000
31	101 / 101	100 / 100	99 / 99	97 / 97	92 / 92	400 / 700	2000 / 2800	3000 / 4000	−1000 / −1700	−4000 / −6000	−9000 / −13000	27	4400	P	0.5m / 0.5m	700 / 1200

* All pecuniary amounts in £ sterling.
† Occupation code: Academic (A), Research Worker (R), Public Sector Employee (P).

137

Mortality tables imply that, on a 'relative frequency' interpretation, the probability of death on any particular day for an individual aged between thirty and thirty-five is about 1/350,000. Assuming that the individual's subjective probabilities of death on either airline may be approximated by the relative frequencies given in the historical accident records, one might therefore estimate $-(\partial v/\partial p)_{\bar{p}}$ for an individual aged about thirty by, for example, dividing the difference between the figure given in question 1(b) and £100 by the corresponding implied change in probability (i.e. 1/500,000). For individuals in the forty-to-fifty-year age bracket, $\bar{p}$ for a given day is closer to 1/100,000, so that in these cases it would probably be preferable to divide the difference between £100 and the figure given in 1(c) by the corresponding implied change in probability (i.e. 3/500,000). These were, in fact, the estimation procedures adopted in those cases in which the relevant fare differences were non-zero and specified. Unfortunately, in some cases the responses to 1(a) and 1(b) were £100, presumably indicating that the subject regarded accident rates of 0, 1 and 2 accidents in 500,000 flights as insignificantly different. In these cases $-(\partial v/\partial p)_{\bar{p}}$ was estimated on the basis of the smallest *non-zero* difference in fares. A similar procedure was adopted for older subjects whose response to 1(c) was 'X'. No attempt was made to estimate $-(\partial v/\partial p)_{\bar{p}}$ if *either* the response to 1(a) or 1(b) was *less* than £100 (in such cases the identification of subjective probabilities with relative frequencies is plainly illegitimate) *or* if the responses changed from '£100' to 'X' with no intermediate values (in such cases the implied $v(p)$ is either a discontinuous function or else such that the 'net' of probabilities in the questionnaire is insufficiently fine to allow estimation of $v(p)$).

The responses to question 3 clearly indicate that the majority of subjects perceived a difference between adding one year to life expectancy and subtracting one year from it and that they preferred the former to the latter. In such cases $(\partial v/\partial \mu)_{\bar{\mu}}$ was estimated simply by dividing the difference between the responses to 3(a) and 3(d) by 2. In those cases in which the responses to 3(a) and 3(d) were identical then, for example, the difference between 3(b) and 3(d) was divided by 6.

Notice that for the majority of respondents the value of $-(\partial v/\partial p)_{\bar{p}}$ implied by the answers to question 2 is very similar to that implied by the answers to question 1. This suggests that, for safety changes effective over relatively short periods, $-(\partial v/\partial p)_{\bar{p}}$ will be only *weakly* affected by the length of the period during which the safety change occurs. This is hardly surprising for the following reasons. The probability, p, of death during (for example) a year conditional on survival to the beginning of that year is given by

$$p = \pi_1 + \pi_2(1 - \pi_1) + \pi_3(1 - \pi_1)(1 - \pi_2)$$
$$+ \ldots \pi_{365}(1 - \pi_1)(1 - \pi_2) \ldots (1 - \pi_{364}) \qquad (6.1)$$

where π_i is the probability of death on the ith day conditional on survival to the beginning of the ith day.

For all π_i small it follows that

$$p \simeq \sum_{i=1}^{365} \pi_i. \qquad (6.2)$$

Now suppose that the individual would forfeit a sum δw to effect a *ceteris paribus* reduction $\delta \pi$ in the probability of death on any particular day. $-(\partial v/\partial p)_{\bar{p}}$ for a time period of one day would then be estimated by $\delta w/\delta \pi$. If, by contrast, the probability change applied to *every* day during the year then, by (6.2), the probability change, δp, for the year would be approximated by $365\delta\pi$. If (as assumed) all $\delta\pi$ are small so that δp is also small *and* $v(p)$ is continuous, then the individual would forfeit approximately $365\delta w$ to effect the probability change δp. Thus $-(\partial v/\partial p)_{\bar{p}}$ for a time period of one year would also be given by

$$\frac{365\delta w}{365\delta \pi} = \frac{\delta w}{\delta p}.$$

The estimates of $-(\partial v/\partial p)_{\bar{p}}$ and $(\partial v/\partial \mu)$ are summarised in histograms in figures 6.1—6.4. Modal values and means are shown in table 6.2.

In section 5.IX it was argued that, for the purposes of a conventional cost—benefit analysis, the value (in addition to avoidance of real resource costs and losses of net output) of an anticipated saving of one (anonymous) life during some forthcoming period is given by the average over the relevant population of the marginal value of a decrease in risk. For the sample of individuals who participated in the experiment, this average is clearly about £3m. It should, however, be noted that this estimate is based upon the marginal values of probability changes effective only for the individual himself. To the extent that probability changes apply to others, and assuming that most individuals will place a positive value upon improvements in the safety of those they care about, the figures given in table 6.2 are clearly an *underestimate* of the relevant

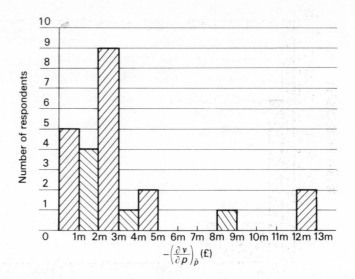

Figure 6.1. Histogram of 'short-period' estimates of $-(\partial v/\partial p)_{\bar{p}}$

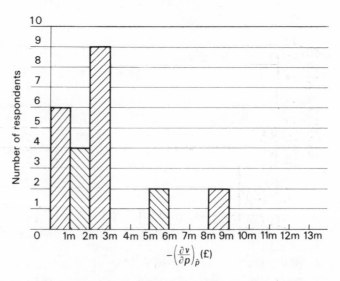

Figure 6.2. Histogram of 'long-period' estimates of $-(\partial v/\partial p)_{\bar{p}}$

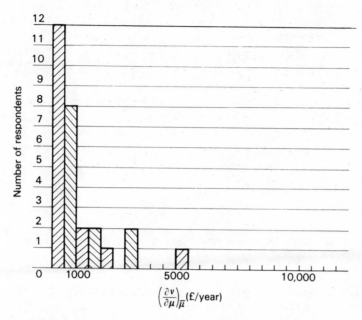

Figure 6.3. Histogram of 'self only' estimates of $(\partial v/\partial \mu)_{\bar{\mu}}$

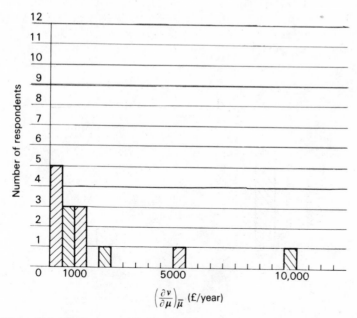

Figure 6.4. Histogram of 'self and family' estimates of $(\partial v/\partial \mu)_{\bar{\mu}}$

Table 6.2

	Mode	Mean
'Short period' estimate of $-\left(\dfrac{\partial v}{\partial p}\right)_{\bar{p}}$	£2–3m.	£3.1m.
'Long period' estimate of $-\left(\dfrac{\partial v}{\partial p}\right)_{\bar{p}}$	£2–3m.	£2.5m.
'Self only' estimate of $\left(\dfrac{\partial v}{\partial \mu}\right)_{\bar{\mu}}$	£0–500/yr	£900/yr
'Self and family' estimate of $\left(\dfrac{\partial v}{\partial \mu}\right)_{\bar{\mu}}$	£0–500/yr	£1790/yr

value. (Presumably the extent of the underestimation can be gauged by comparing the 'self-only' estimate of $(\partial v/\partial \mu)_{\bar{\mu}}$ with the 'self and family' estimate.)

At this stage it is possible to conduct a rudimentary consistency test of the type mentioned in section 6.I. Let us denote by $p_i(i = 1 \ldots T)$ the age-specific probability of death for a particular individual (that is, p_i is the probability of death during the ith year conditional on survival to the beginning of that year) and by $\mu_i(i = 1 \ldots T)$ the individual's age-specific life expectancy (that is, μ_i is the individual's life expectancy conditional on survival to the beginning of the ith year). It then follows *by definition*[6] that

$$\mu_1 \equiv \frac{1p_1}{2} + \frac{3p_2}{2}(1-p_1) + \frac{5p_3}{2}(1-p_2)(1-p_1)$$
$$+ \ldots \frac{(2T-1)p_T}{2}(1-p_{T-1}) \ldots (1-p_1). \qquad (6.3)$$

Thus

$$\frac{\partial \mu_1}{\partial p_1} = \frac{1}{2} - \left[\frac{3p_2}{2} - \frac{5p_3}{2}(1-p_2)\right.$$
$$\left. + \ldots \frac{(2T-1)p_T}{2}(1-p_{T-1}) \ldots (1-p_2)\right] \qquad (6.4)$$

$$= \frac{1}{2} - \left(\frac{1}{2} + \mu_2\right) \qquad (6.5)$$

$$= -\mu_2. \qquad (6.6)$$

But

$$\frac{\partial v}{\partial p_1} = \frac{\partial v}{\partial \mu_1} \frac{\partial \mu_1}{\partial p_1} + \sum_{j=2}^{\infty} \frac{\partial v}{\partial m_j} \frac{\partial m_j}{\partial p_1} \qquad (6.7)$$

where m_j is the jth moment of the density function about the mean.

Since it seems reasonable to suppose that an individual's aversion to an increase, δp_1, in p_1 will be considerably greater than his aversion to the corresponding *ceteris paribus* decrease, $(\partial \mu / \partial p_1)\delta p_1$, in μ_1 alone, the summation term or the right-hand side of (6.7) will be strictly negative so that from (6.7) we can write

$$\left| \frac{\partial v}{\partial p_1} \right| > \left| \frac{\partial v}{\partial \mu_1} \cdot \frac{\partial \mu_1}{\partial p_1} \right| \qquad (6.8)$$

or, from (6.6) and (6.8)

$$\left| \frac{\partial v}{\partial p_1} \right| > \left| -\mu_2 \frac{\partial v}{\partial \mu_1} \right|. \qquad (6.9)$$

One can therefore conduct a simple consistency test on the questionnaire responses by seeing whether or not the implied values for $\partial v/\partial p_1$ and $\partial v/\partial \mu_1$ satisfy (6.9). Since none of the sample respondents had a current age-specific life expectancy exceeding sixty years (and in many cases a considerably smaller figure), this condition is clearly fulfilled by *all* respondents in the sample. However, it must be admitted that in the absence of more specific information concerning

$$\sum_{j=2}^{\infty} \frac{\partial v}{\partial m_j} \frac{\partial m_j}{\partial p_1}$$

the consistency test is *very* weak indeed. None the less, it does serve to illustrate the kind of procedure that may be used to test the veracity of questionnaire responses.

Finally, figures 6.5 and 6.6 show sketches of the graphs of $v(p)$ and $v(\mu)$ implied by the questionnaire answers of a selection of respondents. These tend to confirm the conclusions of chapter 5 concerning the general properties of $v(p)$ and $v(\mu)$.

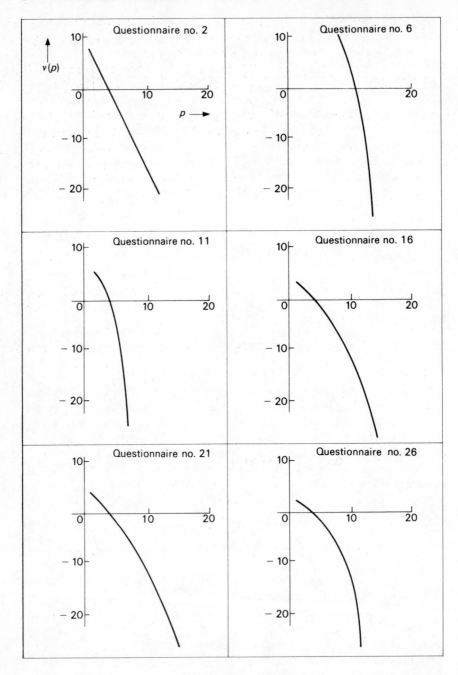

Figure 6.5. Graphs of $v(p)$, 'short-period' ($v(p)$: £; p: 10^{-6})

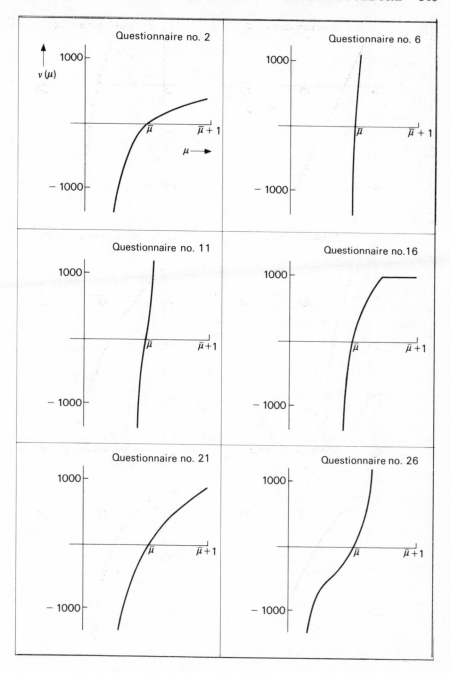

Figure 6.6. Graphs of $v(\mu)$, 'self only' ($v(\mu)$: £; μ: years)

NOTES

1. The conventional procedure for estimating a function such as $L(w)$ is to assign arbitrary values to $L(w)$ for *two* values of w, say w_1 and w_2. Values for $L(w)$ for $w_1 < w < w_2$ are then obtained by discovering the probability at which the individual would be indifferent between w with certainty and a gamble whose alternative outcomes are w_1 and w_2. $L(w)$ is then given by the expected utility for the gamble.

2. A 'universally testable' proposition is one capable in principle of being tested by *anyone*. It would *not*, of course, necessarily be possible to establish the universal *truth* of such a proposition.

3. Notice that such behaviour does not necessarily mean that the individual concerned cannot be treated as an expected utility-maximiser. All that is required for expected utility-maximisation is that the individual behave *as if* he formalised degrees of belief as subjective probabilities and *as if* he obeyed the axioms discussed in chapter 3. The fact that his actual behaviour is more or less instinctive or that he is ignorant of probability concepts is neither here nor there.

4. Following the reservations noted above concerning the capacity of individuals to answer questions of the type posed in the experiment, it must be admitted that this sample is highly biased from the point of view of conventional measures of intelligence, so that members of the sample probably had less difficulty with the conceptual problems presented by the questionnaire than might be experienced by the 'average' layman.

5. In some cases the answers to question 3 were given in *percentage* terms (an early version of the questionnaire did not specify that absolute amounts were required). In such cases the figures which appear in table 6.1 are estimates based on an assumed area A house price of £10,000.

6. Adopting the convention of regarding an individual who dies *during* the ith year as having died precisely half-way through the year, i.e. as having survived for $\frac{1}{2}(2i - 1)$ years from the present time. Notice that we also maintain the convention of treating the Tth year as the latest in which it is regarded as being possible that the individual will still be alive.

7. Summary and Postscript

I SUMMARY OF MAIN RESULTS

This book set out to consider the question of what constitutes an appropriate procedure for placing a value upon the anticipated saving of (typically anonymous) human life or the avoidance of (typically anonymous) human injury. The following are the more important results and conclusions of the analysis.

(a) The constituents of an appropriate valuation procedure are fundamentally conditioned by the intended meaning of the term 'value'. In the context of a conventional cost—benefit analysis the relevant definition of the value (to an individual) of an allocative change is the amount of income or wealth that the individual would forgo to effect the change (i.e. his 'compensating variation' in income or wealth).

(b) An anticipated reduction in the mortality rate during some period of time affords any particular individual *three* major components of value:

(i) a reduction in his share of the real resource costs occasioned by the death of others;

(ii) a reduction in his share of the loss of net output owing to the death of others;

(iii) a reduction in the risk of his own death or the death of anyone he cares about.

Similar comments apply to an anticipated reduction in the non-fatal accident rate.

(c) As far as the existing literature is concerned the most neglected component of value is (iii).

(d) The opportunity to purchase life insurance provides a means of redistributing family wealth between the contingencies of one's own survival or demise. As such, life insurance plays an important, if indirect, part in determining the value of life and safety.

(e) Because of tax allowances on life insurance premia, life insurance may be treated as approximately 'fair'.

(f) Denoting by $L(w)$ the cardinal utility of wealth conditional on survival of a given period of time and by $D(w)$ the cardinal utility of wealth conditional on death during the period, the necessary and sufficient condition for an individual to purchase *some* fair life insurance is

$$\frac{dL}{dw}\bigg|_{w=\bar{w}} < \frac{dD}{dw}\bigg|_{w=\bar{w}}$$

where $\bar{w}$ is the initial level of wealth.

(g) If an individual does purchase fair insurance then he will do so in an amount that satisfies the following condition:

$$\frac{dL}{dw}\bigg|_{w=\bar{w}-x} = \frac{dD}{dw}\bigg|_{w=\bar{w}+z}$$

where x is the insurance premium and z is the net sum assured.

(h) Denoting the cardinal utility of initial wealth w conditional on death at time t by $U(w, t)$, the continuous-time version of the necessary and sufficient condition for an individual to purchase *some* fair life insurance is that *without* insurance $\partial U/\partial w$ should be a decreasing function of t. Similarly, if an individual does purchase life insurance then he will do so in an amount that ensures that $\partial U/\partial w$ becomes independent of t.

(i) Interpreting the risk of death during any period as a *subjective probability*, the value, v, of a change in risk from initial level $\bar{p}$ to some value p is given by a continuous function $v(p)$ having the following properties irrespective of whether or not the individual purchases life insurance:

(i) $p \gtreqless \bar{p} \Rightarrow v(p) \lesseqgtr 0$

(ii) $\dfrac{\partial v}{\partial p} < 0$

(iii) $\dfrac{\partial^2 v}{\partial p^2} < 0.$

(iv) For some individuals there will exist a value of p *strictly less than unity* for which $v(p) = -\infty$.

(j) Since most safety improvements will afford only very small decreases in individual risk, for policy purposes the most important concept in evaluating the desirability of a single-period safety improvement is the 'marginal value of a decrease in risk' (at the initial risk level) denoted by $-(\partial v/\partial p)_{\bar{p}}$. The marginal value of a decrease in risk has been shown to be a *non-increasing* function of initial risk (strictly decreasing if the individual holds no life insurance) and an *increasing* function of initial wealth.

(k) Taking a 'long' view, and considering changes in safety effective over an individual's entire lifetime, the natural interpretation of an increase in safety is an increase in *longevity*, or more formally an increase in *life expectancy* (i.e. an increase in the mathematical expectation of age at death.) The value, v, of an increase in life expectancy, μ, from initial level $\bar{\mu}$ is given by a continuous function $v(\mu)$ having the following properties irrespective of whether or not the individual purchases life insurance:

(i) $\mu \gtreqqless \bar{\mu} \Rightarrow v(\mu) \gtreqqless 0$

(ii) $\dfrac{\partial v}{\partial \mu} > 0$

(iii) $\dfrac{\partial^2 v}{\partial \mu^2} < 0$

(iv) For some individuals there will exist a non-zero value of μ for which $v(\mu) = -\infty$.

(l) Since most safety improvements will afford only very small increases in individual life expectancy, for policy purposes the most important concept in evaluating the desirability of a safety improvement effective over an extended time horizon is the marginal value of an increase in life expectancy, $(dv/d\mu)_{\bar{\mu}}$. This marginal value is a *decreasing* function of initial life expectancy, $\bar{\mu}$, and an *increasing* function of initial wealth.

(m) Most of the above results also apply to variations in the risk of non-fatal injury and 'indirect'[1] risks.

(n) If value is given the alternative interpretation as an 'equivalent variation' in income or wealth (i.e. as the sum that an individual would require to compensate for failure to make an allocative adjustment) then the marginal value of a change in risk (as a variation in either p or μ) is *precisely the same* as that given by the 'compensating variation' definition of value.

(o) For the purposes of cost—benefit analysis the appropriate value to place upon the anticipated saving of one (anonymous) life during a particular time period is (in addition to avoidance of real resource costs and losses of net output) given by the average, over the relevant population, of the marginal value of a decrease in risk. In so far as the concept of a 'value of life' has any relevance in the analysis of safety improvement this is the appropriate interpretation of such a concept. Other definitions of the 'value of life', such as the present value of anticipated future output *per capita* or court awards to the relatives of accident victims, are quite irrelevant for conventional cost—benefit analysis.

(p) Empirical evidence suggests that *the average 'marginal value of a decrease in risk' for risk changes effective over relatively short periods of time has an order of magnitude in excess of £3m.* and as such is many multiples of the figure currently being used in public sector decision-making in the UK to value the anticipated saving of a life.[2]

II   SOME POLICY IMPLICATIONS

It is not the primary purpose of this book to make policy recommendations concerning allocative and investment decisions in the public sector, but rather to provide an analytical apparatus by which such decisions may be facilitated. None the less, some of the results of the analysis have such strong and immediate implications for policy that it seems worth underlining and emphasising the relevant points.

(a) Subject to all of the reservations noted in sections 5.III and 5.VI, the results concerning the relationship between the marginal value of a decrease in risk and the level of initial risk suggests that a given risk reduction for a high-risk section of society will have a higher value than the same risk reduction for similarly sized low-risk section of society, *ceteris paribus*. This suggests that a socially optimal arrangement will be characterised by an equalisation of risks among various sections of the community.

(b) Given that risk reduction is a non-inferior good, the value of safety improvement will tend to be an increasing function of the aggregate wealth of the group whose safety is affected. Needless to say, any policy inference will be tempered by distributional considerations.

(c) If, as the results of chapter 6 suggest, the average 'marginal value of a decrease in risk' is many multiples of the value currently being placed upon an anticipated saving of one life during the relevant time period, then it appears that the analysis has produced *prima facie* evidence of a severe underexpenditure on safety and longevity-improvement.[3]

III SOME POSSIBLE OBJECTIONS TO THE METHOD OF ANALYSIS

There are two quite distinct grounds on which it is possible to object to the argument developed in this book. In the first place, one might not subscribe to the particular view of cost—benefit analysis adopted as a basis for the entire analysis. It can be argued, for example, that the inherent defects of the potential Pareto improvement criterion (and in particular its failure to confront distributional issues) are such as to render it virtually worthless as a decision-making tool. None the less, even if this position is adopted, it seems rather unlikely that whatever allocative rule is used instead will completely *ignore* private preferences. This being the case, our analysis — concentrating as it does upon the individual's own valuation of changes in his safety and longevity — must surely continue to have relevance for policy formation. Indeed, it should be stressed that at no stage has it been argued that a positive aggregate-compensating variation should be regarded as the *sole* reason for advocating a particular allocative adjustment. In a sense the avoidance of distributional questions is at once the limitation and the strength of an analysis such as that developed in this book.

However, even if one believes that we have asked the right kind of questions for policy purposes, it may nevertheless be argued that these questions have been answered in an inappropriate way, because of deficiencies either in the theoretical or empirical analysis.

As far as the theoretical analysis is concerned, the most obvious potential criticism is that individuals will typically not display sufficient order and consistency in choice situations to make expected utility maximisation a legitimate hypothesis for present purposes. Indeed, there exist well-known paradoxes in which the majority of individuals violate one or more of the axioms from which the Expected Utility Theorem is derived.[4] However, if individual choice under uncertainty is to be taken to display any order and consistency at all — and it seems necessary to assume that it does if we are to make any progress with our problem — then by any of the criteria that might be thought relevant in judging the quality of a theory, the expected utility-maximisation hypothesis seems to do pretty well, and certainly better than any rival theory, if we consider its overall performance. For example consider the following (non-exhaustive) list of characteristics that are commonly considered desirable in a theory (apart from the obvious prerequisites of logically consistent assumptions and logically valid derivations of theorems):

(a) explanatory power;
(b) generality (including the capacity to explain and interrelate a wide range of apparently diverse empirical phenomena);
(c) predictive capacity (i.e. the generation of empirically falsifiable, *but as yet unfalsified* propositions of the form 'there is a high likelihood that events of type A, B, C . . . etc. will be associated [often temporally followed by] events of type $\alpha, \beta, \Gamma \ldots$ etc.');
(d) simplicity and comprehensibility;
(e) *a priori* appeal of the theory's assumptions (i.e. that the latter should afford a 'satisfactory' description of the phenomena which the theory is about);
(f) consistency with other theories which have so far not been irremediably refuted or supplanted by 'superior' theories.

Together with weak assumptions concerning, for example, properties of utility of wealth functions, the expected utility-maximisation hypothesis clearly scores well in any sensible overal weighting of these performance criteria and it is therefore hardly surprising that it is by far the most popular theoretical foundation for the analysis of choice under uncertainty. There are, however, two important reservations that should be noted. The first concerns the assumption of concavity of the conditional utility of wealth functions embodied in (4.11) and (4.13). This assumption implies financial risk aversion, which appears to be *consistent* with observed choices concerning insurance, asset portfolio diversification and small bets, but *inconsistent* with the observed prevalence of willingness to undertake less than fair bets having small stakes and a small probability of very large gains.[5] Quite apart from the fact that it is possible to eliminate the inconsistency by postulating that large bet behaviour is merely a manifestation of bettor-optimism (reflected in subjective probabilities of winning, which exceed relative frequencies), the problem does not seem serious from our point of view. This is because we have been primarily concerned with the life insurance decision and with the *marginal* value of a change in risk, the latter involving the properties of the utility of wealth function *only* in the neighbourhood of initial wealth.[6]

The second reservation concerning the expected utility hypothesis is associated with the *subjective* (as opposed to the objective, or relative, frequency) interpretation of probability. This arises from the fact that subjective probabilities are strictly non-observable, and therefore non-empirical phenomena. Consequently if the expected utility-maximisation hypothesis is to be given operational content it is necessary to specify the relationship between subjective probabilities of events and certain *observable* characteristics of the situation or mechanism which determines which event will occur. This means, in particular, that all of the results of chapter 5 should (strictly speaking) be supplemented by a specification of precisely *how* a change in safety will affect the subjective probabilities of death or injury. While it seems very reasonable to assume that an improvement in safety will cause subjective probabilities to decrease, it is far less clear how one is to *quantify* these decreases in any particular set of circumstances. This problem causes difficulty at two stages in the analysis. In the first place it will be recalled that in the empirical estimation of, for example, $v(p)$ it was assumed that subjective probabilities could be identified with relative frequencies. Is this reasonable? Perhaps the only defence one can offer is that there seems to be no reason to suppose that, over a large sample of individuals, there will be a *systematic* divergence between subjective probabilities and relative frequencies when information concerning the latter is available to individual decision-makers. The subjective probability concept also raises difficulties in the *use* of the empirical estimates of $v(p)$ in allocative decision-making. Suppose that the social decision-maker believes that a particular safety improvement will save s lives in a population N during some future period of time. Is it then legitimate to suppose that each member of the relevant population will (as assumed in section 5.IX) adjust his degree of belief in the event of his own death to an extent which can be precisely described as a reduction of s/N in the subjective probability of the event? This does seem rather unlikely. What then is the decision-maker to do? It might be argued that, since he has access to information and technical advice (concerning the extent of the safety improvement) not typically available to individuals in the affected group, he should work on the assumption that these individuals would arrive at similar views to his own concerning the probability change if they *did* have access to such information and advice. The problem with this approach is that it does, strictly speaking, violate the precept that 'individuals are the best judges of their own welfare' upon which the potential Pareto improvement criterion was founded. (It will be recalled that a conventional cost—benefit analysis is ultimately a test of whether or not a particular allocative change implies a potential Pareto improvement — i.e. whether with redistribution an actual Pareto improvement is achievable — and that a Pareto improvement is simply a change in which some individuals regard themselves as gainers while none regard themselves as losers).

The operative term is 'regard themselves', the point being that on a strict interpretation of the potential Pareto improvement criterion the relevant question is whether individuals *actually do* feel better off rather than whether they *would* feel better off if they were as well informed as the social decision-maker. Advocates of this view would argue that it is completely irrelevant that the social decision-maker regards individual evaluation of the desirability of a safety improvement as being based upon a misconception of the extent of the improvement: he is notwithstanding obliged (for the purposes of cost—benefit analysis) to take account *only* of individuals' evaluations of their *own* perceptions of the degree of safety improvement.

A possible reconciliation of these opposing views lies in recognition of the existence of information costs. If information dissemination was costless then a feasible and apparently attractive course of action for the social decision-maker would be to ensure that individuals have access to all relevant information concerning a proposed safety improvement. It would then not be unreasonable for him to assume that their assessments of the probability change would tend to coincide with his own. But of course information dissemination is *not* costless, nor for that matter is the *interpretation* of information, especially if the latter is of a rather technical nature. Given these points there is certainly a case to be made for basing a cost—benefit analysis upon estimates of the individual valuations that *would* prevail in a hypothetical *fully informed* world.[7]

There is another problem associated with the use of estimates of $v(p)$ and $v(\mu)$ in policy formation which deserves mention at this stage. This problem arises because the analysis has not explicitly considered an individual's opportunity to influence his own safety either by changes in care or by expenditure on *marketed* safety improvement devices. The existence of such opportunities may mean that an individual will react to a probability reduction from $\bar{p}$ to p by taking less (or more) care and/or by spending less (or more) on private safety improvement, so that the *net* change in safety is different from $\bar{p}$ to p. However it is clear that the amount that an individual would forfeit for an immutable risk reduction from $\bar{p}$ to p cannot be less than he would forfeit for the same reduction given the opportunity to indulge in subsequent private risk adjustment. $v(p)$ and $v(\mu)$ will therefore tend to *underestimate* the value of safety improvement when such opportunities exist but will do so to a negligible extent if, as seems likely, private adjustments are small relative to the initial safety improvement.

Objections to the empirical estimation procedure are probably the most difficult to deal with. As already noted, what is ideally required is an estimate of $v(p)$ (or $v(\mu)$) based on actual choices from real alternatives. Instead the estimates in chapter 6 were derived from imagined, deliberate responses to hypothetical situations. In addition, as already noted, it was necessary to assume that subjective probabilities could be identified with relative frequencies. Chapter 6 began with a careful defence of these procedures and this defence will not be rehearsed in detail here. Suffice it to say that, *if* one believes that quantitative information concerning private valuation is important for public policy formation and *if* for various reasons it is not feasible to obtain estimates from (e.g.) market data, *then* there remain just two alternatives: to do nothing, or to proceed by questionnaire. The usefulness of the estimates in chapter 6 is premised in the belief that the results of individuals' deliberative, cognitive evaluations of hypothetical alternatives will at least give an indication of the *order of magnitude* of the marginal values of safety implied by possibly unconscious, instinctive choices among real alternatives. This belief is in turn founded in the view that there is no convincing reason for supposing that the responses to a questionnaire will give a *systematically* biased estimate of the 'true' value. After all, most forms of forethought and contingency planning require us to introspect about 'what we would do if . . .'. Are we to suppose that such speculation is always, or even predominantly, infected with pessimism (or optimism)? One doubts that this is so. It might of course be argued that the *type* of speculation required is so unusual as to render its results of doubtful relevance as indicators of how people would in fact choose. This is probably the nub of the problem and it is here that one must simply decide whether or not questionnaire results are to be taken seriously. Those who believe that they are will, like the author, wish to know why the order of magnitude of the implied value of saving a life is so many multiples of the figure currently being used in allocative decision-making and will regard this divergence as *prima facie* evidence of misallocation. Sceptics will, by contrast, presumably be unperturbed.

Finally, a criticism that applies both to the theoretical and empirical analyses is that throughout the discussion death has been treated as an *unique* event. The limitation of this approach is that most people would presumably prefer to die quickly and painlessly rather than slowly and painfully, so that ideally one ought to distinguish various kinds of death. This problem does not seem serious for the theoretical analysis provided that the results of the latter are treated as applying to variations in the risk of any *particular* way of dying. However, in the case of the empirical analysis the results of the experiment should strictly be taken as applying *only* to the modes of death implied by the questionnaire. Despite this reservation, the purpose of the exercise was merely to indicate orders of magnitude and as such it is probably adequate to assume, for example, that while answers to the first part of the questionnaire are directly relevant to 'quick painless' death (by airline accident) they none the less give an indication of the lower bound of the value of variations in the risk of more unpleasant ways of dying.

IV   SOME UNRESOLVED PROBLEMS

While the analysis developed in earlier chapters has provided a conceptual framework for considering the value of changes in safety and longevity, and has also generated a number of interesting qualitative and quantitative results, there are some important directions in which further fruitful development might be possible.

At the purely theoretical level, the continuous time analysis dealt only with changes in life expectancy: it would certainly be interesting to investigate the private valuation of changes in other parameters of the probability density function, $\rho(t)$. For example, how would individuals react to a reduction in the variance of $\rho(t)$ reflecting, presumably, greater certainty concerning the time of death? Throughout the analysis it has been assumed that insurance may be treated as fair: how would relaxation of this assumption affect the results? On the basis of the relatively weak restrictions on the various conditional utility functions, it seems that the results would hold for variation 'in the region of fairness', but what of larger variations? Is it possible to develop a more specific set of results for the value of variation in indirect risks and the risk of non-fatal injury than those presented in section 5.VII? How might one incorporate the phenomenon of private risk adjustment mentioned in section 7.III? These and many other interesting questions have not been answered in this book simply because unequivocal answers appear to require stronger *a priori* restrictions on the properties of, in particular, utility functions than seemed appropriate in what is intended as a *general* theoretical framework. This is not to deny that further restrictions might be defensible on *a priori* or empirical grounds. One simply hopes that what has been done here will stimulate others to provide cogent and persuasive justification for such restrictions.

Perhaps the richest vein of potential for further work lies in the empirical estimation of functions such as $v(p)$ and $v(\mu)$, and the associated marginal values of safety improvement. Apart from extension and refinement of the estimation methods discussed in chapter 6, a tempting alternative avenue of approach is obviously the inference of the forms of these functions from data concerning actual choice. This type of approach was not employed in chapter 6 simply because of doubts about the adequacy of currently available data. However this is not to say that such data are *inherently* unobtainable, one possibility being to collect them 'from scratch' by careful observation of the kinds of tradeoff that people make in risky occupations.[8]

V   CONCLUDING COMMENTS

The rationale for the argument developed in this book is rooted in two implicit fundamental postulates:

(a) that it is a fact of life that society confronts a problem of scarcity and must in consequence engage in continual allocative choices; and

(b) that in so far as such choices occur in the public sector, it is desirable that those who make them should do so on the basis of more rather than less information concerning private preferences.

If these two premises are granted, then it must at least be conceded that the problem considered in this book has substantial social relevance. Whether the problem has been confronted in an appropriate and fruitful way is a matter for the reader to judge. However, if the argument has done no more than stimulate a critical interest, map out key issues and offer a few tentative answers, then the author will be well satisfied.

NOTES

1. In the sense of the term employed by Mishan (see section 2.VII).
2. The figure in current use (1974) in the UK is basically an updated version of the Dawson (1971) estimate based on gross rather than net output (see section 2.VI), the total value per life saved being £26,000.

3. Furthermore, recall that it was argued in sections 2.XIII and 5.IX that the *total ex-ante* value per life saved will comprise the average (over the relevant population) of the marginal value of a decrease in risk *plus* real resource cost and net output—loss savings. Using Dawson's (1967) estimates updated to 1974 prices, the average real resource cost and net output—loss savings due to the avoidance of one death total about £6000, so that according to the estimates of the average marginal value of a decrease in risk given in chapter 6, the latter represents the *overwhelmingly predominant* component of the total value per life saved.

4. See, for example, Markowitz (1959) p. 218.

5. See, for example, Friedman and Savage (1948) and Markowitz (1952).

6. In the insured case this should be interpreted as *conditional* initial wealth.

7. Underlying this argument there is, of course, the value judgement that it is desirable that individuals should have access to as much information as possible (*ceteris paribus*) concerning safety improvements. While this position has a certain immediate appeal it is worth noting that the desirability of information is not always unequivocal. Suppose, for example, that additional information (concerning, say, the danger of smoking) will not cause an individual to alter his behaviour but will make him feel less happy. It is then not at all clear that it is a 'good thing' to bring such information to his attention. (I am grateful to John Kay for bringing this point to *my* attention.)

8. This is, indeed, broadly speaking the kind of approach employed by Melinek (see section 2.X above). However in order to meet the objections noted in section 2.XIII it would seem necessary to have access to a rather richer body of data than that employed by Melinek.

REFERENCES

Dawson, R. F. F. *Cost of Road Accidents in Great Britain*, London, Road Research Laboratory, Ministry of Transport (1967).

Dawson, R. F. F. *Current Costs of Road Accidents in Great Britain*, London, Road Research Laboratory, Ministry of Transport (1971).

Friedman, M. and Savage, L. J. 'The Utility Analysis of Choices Involving Risk' *Journal of Political Economy* (August 1948)

Markowitz, H. 'The Utility of Wealth' *Journal of Political Economy* (April 1952)

Markowitz, H. *Portfolio Selection* New York, Wiley (1959)

Index